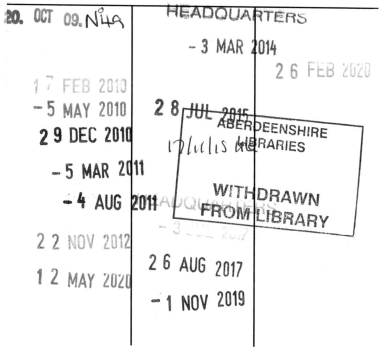
LEE, John

The gas attacks, Ypres 1915

The Gas Attacks
Ypres 1915

Campaign Chronicles

The Gas Attacks Ypres 1915

John Lee

—➤-◦-◄—

Campaign Chronicles
Series Editor

Christopher Summerville

Pen & Sword
MILITARY

For my dear wife, Celia
A fellow historian and biographer

First published in Great Britain in 2009 by
Pen & Sword Military
an imprint of
Pen & Sword Books Ltd
47 Church Street
Barnsley
South Yorkshire
S70 2AS

Copyright © John Lee, 2009

ISBN 978 1 84415 929 1

Pen & Sword Books Ltd incorporates the imprints of
Pen & Sword Aviation, Pen & Sword Family History, Pen & Sword Maritime,
Pen & Sword Military, Wharncliffe Local History, Pen & Sword Select,
Pen & Sword Military Classics, Leo Cooper, Remember When,
Seaforth Publishing and Frontline Publishing.

For a complete list of Pen & Sword titles please contact
PEN & SWORD BOOKS LIMITED
47 Church Street, Barnsley, South Yorkshire, S70 2AS, England
E-mail: enquiries@pen-and-sword.co.uk
Website: www.pen-and-sword.co.uk

Contents

List of Illustrations

List of Abbreviations

BEF	British Expeditionary Force
CEF	Canadian Expeditionary Force
C-in-C	Commander-in-Chief
CO	Commanding Officer
CSM	Company Sergeant Major
DCLI	Duke of Cornwall's Light Infantry
DLI	Durham Light Infantry
FA	Field Artillery
GHQ	General Headquarters
GS	General Service
HE	High Explosive
HLI	Highland Light Infantry
KOSB	King's Own Scottish Borderers
KOYLI	King's Own Yorkshire Light Infantry
KRRC	King's Royal Rifle Corps
KSLI	King's Shropshire Light Infantry
MC	Military Cross
MM	Military Medal
NCO	Non Commissioned Officer
NF	Northumberland Fusiliers
PPCLI	Princess Patricia's Canadian Light Infantry
R	Royal
RAMC	Royal Army Medical Corps
RB	Rifle Brigade
RE	Royal Engineers
RF	Royal Fusiliers
RFA	Royal Field Artillery
RGA	Royal Garrison Artillery
RHA	Royal Horse Artillery
RSM	Regimental Sergeant Major
SLI	Somerset Light Infantry
VC	Victoria Cross

Acknowledgements

As I worked on the research for this book I realised there was no useful one-volume study in English of this extraordinary battle at the operational and battalion level that interests me most. My thanks go to Rupert Harding for commissioning what turned out to be a fascinating topic, Chris Summerville for his patient and masterful copy-editing and Pamela Covey for her proofreading services.

The library staff at the Imperial War Museum and National Army Museum were as helpful as we have all come to expect. A special thank you to Tony Cowan for that last-minute book I needed to finish the 'liquid fire' section, and to Simon Jones for his help on the finer points of gas warfare.

My friends and colleagues in the British Commission for Military History and the Western Front Association are a constant source of stimulation and information. Geoff Noon's talk on gas warfare shows what an enormous subject it really is.

Finally Dr Yigal Sheffy who, by asking me for some help on the possible use of the gas weapon at Gallipoli, helped me to conclude that the Western Allies could claim the moral high ground on this thorny issue. Poison gas would not have been used if the Germans had not done so first.

The Gas Attacks: Ypres 1915

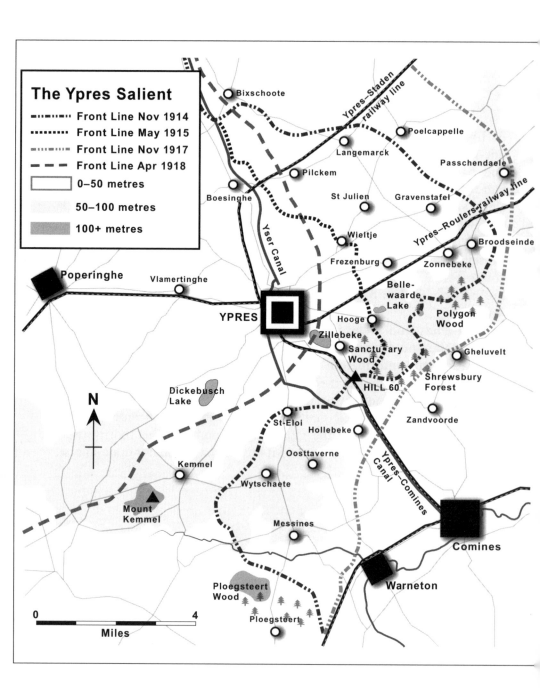

The Ypres Salient

- ···•··· Front Line Nov 1914
- ········ Front Line May 1915
- ···•··· Front Line Nov 1917
- – – – Front Line Apr 1918
- ☐ 0–50 metres
- ☐ 50–100 metres
- ▨ 100+ metres

Bixschoote

Ypres–Staden railway line

Poelcappelle

Langemarck

Passchendaele

Pilckem

Boesinghe

St Julien

Gravenstafel

Ypres–Roulers railway line

Yser Canal

Wieltje

Frezenburg

Zonnebeke

Broodseinde

Poperinghe

Vlamertinghe

Belle-
waarde
Lake

Polygon
Wood

YPRES

Hooge

Zillebeke

Gheluvelt

Sanctuary
Wood

Shrewsbury
Forest

HILL 60

N

Dickebusch
Lake

Zandvoorde

St-Eloi

Hollebeke

Oosttaverne

Ypres–Comines
Canal

Kemmel

Wytschaete

Mount
Kemmel

Messines

Comines

Ploegsteert
Wood

Warneton

Ploegsteert

0   4
Miles

Background

It is very hard to find a military justification for the stubborn defence by the Western Allies of the Salient that wrapped around the Belgian town of Ypres. By its very nature a salient is exposed to fire from three sides, and the Germans held the high ground that made sure they had maximum advantage of the situation. If truth be told, there was a range of very significant hills a few miles to the south-west that could have combined to make a formidable defence line that would have been easier to hold and with less troops than were committed to the infamous Ypres Salient.

But war is a political act, and the demands of politics often oblige soldiers to carry out missions of which they might otherwise disapprove. For the Allies to abandon this last corner of Belgium to the invader would have been intolerable and damaging to Allied prestige throughout the world. Ypres would be defended, regardless of the cost. Having gone to war in August 1914 ostensibly to defend the 'scrap of paper' treaty that guaranteed Belgium's independence, the British felt a particular need to stand by their little ally in this last parcel of 'free Belgium'.

October 1914

German cavalry passed through Ypres on 7 October 1914 but did not stay long. On 14 October Lieutenant General Henry Rawlinson's IV Corps (Capper's 7th British and Byng's 3rd Cavalry Divisions), no longer needed at their first destination, Antwerp, occupied Ypres and took up positions some 5 or 6 miles to the east. The British Commander-in-Chief, Sir John French, had finally convinced his French counterpart, Marshal Joffre, to allow the British Expeditionary Force to redeploy from the trench deadlock

1

Sir John French (1852–1925)

Born the son of a naval officer, John French joined the Royal Navy in 1866 before transferring to 8th Hussars in 1874. He served in the Sudan 1884–1885, and led 1st Cavalry Brigade effectively in the Boer war 1899–1901. He was C-in-C Aldershot Command 1901–1907; Inspector General of the Army 1907–1912; Chief of the Imperial General Staff 1912–1914; and was made a Field Marshal in 1913. He resigned as CIGS over the 'Curragh Mutiny' of 1914 but later that year commanded the BEF sent to the Western Front.

His early enthusiasm for the offensive received a shock when he was forced to retreat after the Battle of Mons and relations with his French allies came under a strain. Still more did his two corps commanders find him difficult to work with. In particular Sir Horace Smith-Dorrien was severely criticised for his decision to stand and fight the pursuing Germans at Le Cateau. French became despondent and would have taken the BEF out of the fighting line altogether had not Lord Kitchener intervened to stop him.

He led the BEF through the battles of the Marne, the Aisne, and First Ypres in 1914, and from Neuve Chapelle to Loos in 1915. At Second Ypres he was under the spell of Ferdinand Foch and insisted on very costly counter-attacks to no avail. He took his revenge on Smith-Dorrien during the fighting at Second Ypres, dismissing him for making suggestions that were acted upon as soon as he was gone. His poor handling of reserves during the Battle of Loos, following his courting of the Press during disputes over the provision of shells to the BEF, made him something of a marked man.

French was replaced by Sir Douglas Haig in December 1915 and returned to England to serve as C-in-C Home Forces 1916–1918. He published the vindictive account of '1914'; was Lord Lieutenant of Ireland 1918–1921; and was created Earl of Ypres in 1922. French died in 1925.

along the Aisne to the open country of the Flanders plain. Smith-Dorrien's II Corps, Allenby's Cavalry Corps, Pulteney's III Corps, Haig's I Corps and the Indian Corps arrived, in that order, ostensibly to conduct an offensive around the German right flank. Instead they ran into a massive enemy offensive that had the Channel ports as an objective.

The subsequent fighting was of a particularly desperate nature. Any efforts by the British and French at resuming the offensive were soon defeated. Instead the Western Allies found themselves thrown onto the defensive and battered by powerful German attacks. Germany's War Minister, von Falkenhayn, had, on his own initiative, ordered the creation of six new reserve corps soon after the war began. When he replaced Helmuth von Moltke as Chief of the Great General Staff, Falkenhayn deployed Fourth and Sixth Armies, reinforced by four of the new reserve corps, against this truly decisive objective. Seizing the Channel ports would seriously disrupt Britain's assistance to France.

This scheme was defeated by the Belgian decision to open the sea sluices and inundate the coastal hinterland, undoing centuries of land reclamation. Totally frustrated in the north, the whole weight of the German offensive then fell upon Ypres and, fighting in its defence, the old British Regular Army was effectively destroyed. The skills of the British Regulars, together with the natural stubbornness of their race, and a lot of help from the French and Belgians, fought the Germans to a standstill. A pronounced salient formed around beleaguered Ypres. On more than one occasion the Germans seemed poised on the edge of a great breakthrough, only for some tiny force to intervene at a delicate moment to save the day. One unfortunate 'lesson learned' by the British High Command from this fighting was the need to persist with attacks, even when things appeared hopeless, for the enemy may have no reserves to hand and could be on the brink of defeat. From 1915 to 1917 Allied offensives would run up enormous casualty lists with this 'lesson' in mind.

After the last German attacks in mid-November were defeated, the British Expeditionary Force left the Ypres Salient to the French and Belgians, and took post further south. It was a bitter irony that a few days after they returned in April 1915, the 'quiet' Salient was to be the scene of fighting every bit as savage as the previous autumn and winter.

The Gas Attacks: Ypres 1915

Deadlock on the Western Front . . .

For Germany the war in 1914 was a great disappointment. The plan to defeat France swiftly, and then turn their full attention against Russia, had failed. German forces were firmly ensconced in most of Belgium and in huge and valuable swathes of Northern France. The war there had taken on a wholly unfamiliar aspect – trench deadlock from the Swiss border to the North Sea. This posed, for both sides, a new set of tactical and strategic problems to be worked out as huge new armies had to be organised, equipped and trained for the long haul. The demands on industry were staggering, as pre-war ammunition stocks designed to last for several months were consumed in as many weeks. All the belligerent powers found themselves grappling with new, complex and unforeseen difficulties.

In the East, the unexpectedly speedy Russian invasion of East Prussia had been decisively defeated, but Germany's Austro-Hungarian allies had taken a terrible beating and demanded more and more assistance. The accession of Turkey as an ally might, at least, distract the Western Allies from concentrating all their efforts on the Western Front.

. . . And Possible Ways to Break it

Scientists and inventors of all nations began to address the peculiarities of the trench deadlock. Some would consider the use of lachrymatory agents (tear gas), others the more lethal asphyxiating gases, to clear the enemy trenches of defenders and restore the war of movement to which everyone aspired. Though the gas weapon did not exist as a viable munition anywhere in the world in 1899, at the first Hague Peace Conference the final convention declared: 'The Contracting Powers agree to abstain from the use of all projectiles the sole object of which is the diffusion of asphyxiating or deleterious gases.' The United States of America was the only delegation to abstain from this clause. It was therefore a case of special pleading for German apologists to later argue that a gas cloud was outside the remit of a ban on gas projectiles. Furthermore, the second Hague Convention in 1907 repeated the ban on projectiles of weapons that might cause 'unnecessary suffering', and Article XXIIIa prohibited the use of 'poison or poisoned weapons'. By 1914 the USA had ratified the treaty; only

Italy failed to do so. It was known that the French had developed a concentrated form of tear gas that had supposedly been used in 1912 to storm the headquarters of a French criminal gang. The French Army adapted this gas into special hand grenades for use in clearing fortifications and they were available at the outbreak of war, and improved versions were developed by January 1915. It seems there were plans to use tear gas hand grenades in the French spring offensive in 1915, but they were in the process of manufacture and wouldn't be ready until 15 May. That the French Army ordered 90,000 goggles to protect the eyes only makes it clear that asphyxiating gas was not on the agenda.

When the British War Office made a tentative pre-war enquiry of the Foreign Office whether it was permissible under the second Hague Convention to employ 'preparations giving rise to disagreeable fumes without causing permanent harm' they were firmly told that it was out of the question. In September 1914 both the War Office and the Admiralty specifically prohibited the use of tear gas in shells. Late in 1914 British scientists, based at Imperial College London, began testing various substances for use as a lachrymatory gas. A grenade version was tested in January 1915; a 4.5-inch howitzer shell was ready by March 1915; chemical smoke screens were tested on 9 April. Maurice Hankey, Secretary to the Committee of Imperial Defence, suggested the War Office organise the study of chemical warfare with the express purpose of being ready to retaliate if the Germans used it first.

The Germans had added a gas irritant to some of their artillery shells as early as October 1914, but the British troops against whom it was used near Neuve Chapelle simply didn't notice its effects. The Tappen brothers, one a chemist in the Heavy Artillery Department of the War Ministry and one Chief of the Operations Branch at General Headquarters, developed tear gas shells for the German artillery. These 'T-shells' (named after the Tappens) were first used at Bolimov in Poland on 31 January 1915. The liquid content failed to vaporise in the intense cold and the experiment was a failure. A slightly improved version, with the addition of bromacetone to prevent the problem, was apparently used against French troops on the Belgian coast in March 1915 without any discernible effect, and without the 'victims' noticing anything much. Some experiments were made mixing phosgene with the tear gas to increase its toxicity. Separate trials were held with trench mortar bombs containing a phosgene/chlorine mixture. Scientists were killed and injured in these tests, but the gunners who were expected to use these materials remained lukewarm to the idea. Already a general shortage of artillery shells impinged on the future development of this weapon.

Enter Fritz Haber and 'Disinfection'

In January 1915, while wrestling with the problem of a shell shortage, Falkenhayn received a proposition from Professor Fritz Haber, Director of the Kaiser Wilhelm Institute for Physical Chemistry in Berlin, which suggested that the mighty German chemical industry could provide cylinders of liquid chlorine that could, as a vaporised gas, be released in clouds to drift over the enemy trenches. Haber was a very ambitious and patriotic Prussian citizen. His son (L. F. Haber) describes him as marked by 'strong purpose, great energy, a practical turn of mind, and an outstanding administrative ability'. Clearly lacking any moral reservations on the matter, he simply saw his suggestion and the subsequent work perfecting it as a technical problem to be solved by German industry. He must have known that when chlorine combines with water – and the human body is 80 per cent water – it forms hydrochloric (muracic) acid that would have the most devastating effect on the lungs, eyes and mucous membranes. Falkenhayn immediately approved trials of this lethal weapon, under the chilling codeword 'Disinfection'. Haber was promoted from an NCO to a captain in the Reserve. An initial unit of 500 'gas pioneers' in two companies under Colonel Petersen was soon expanded into Pioneer Regiment 35, 1,600 strong. Organised in two battalions, a number of future distinguished scientists served in its ranks. Special technical and meteorological sections were added. Casualties were incurred in training for the unit. Haber himself was hospitalised after riding into a gas pocket on the great Belgian training grounds at Beverloo on 2 April 1915. The requisitioning of 6,000 cylinders (half the total available in the country), each holding 88lb of liquid chlorine, was followed by the ordering of 24,000 cylinders for 44lb loads. A firm decision was taken to test this new weapon against the southern face of the Ypres Salient, based on the expectation of favourable winds in the early spring.

Background

The Decision to use Poison Gas

From December 1914 the German Fourth Army, commanded by Duke Albrecht of Württemberg, had been considering an attack to eliminate the Ypres Salient, which it always looked upon as a threatening point from which the Allies could develop offensives towards Brussels or Lille. XXIII and XXVI Reserve Corps were already working on plans for an attack that would include the canal, and the Langemarck–Pilckem area, very similar to the actual battle launched on 22 April. Falkenhayn seized upon the idea of using the gas weapon as a diversion to cover the removal of troops from the West to the East. On 25 January 1915 General von Deimling, GOC XV Corps, was told that he would oversee the first attack, somewhere between St Eloi and Gheluvelt, where it was thought the winds would be most favourable. The installation of the gas cylinders, each weighing 187lb, was completed by 10 March 1915. Deimling asked for extra artillery ammunition to exploit a possible breakthrough, but was told that the attack was only in the nature of a trial. If he needed more ammunition it might follow at a later date. A huge programme of improvements to road and rail links, bridges, barracks and training grounds was embarked upon.

There were objections to the new weapon. Deimling himself had strong moral objections to using poison gas. 'The mission of poisoning the enemy as one would rats affected me as it would any straightforward soldier. I was disgusted.' Instead he hoped it would bring a successful conclusion to the deadlock on the Western Front. 'If these poison gases were to bring about the fall of Ypres, perhaps the victory would decide the whole campaign. Faced with such a possibility it was necessary to suppress one's personal feelings. We had to go on, come what may.' Colonel General von Einem, Third Army, expressed his feelings in a letter to his wife, warning of a counter-productive worldwide scandal. The commander of Sixth German Army, Crown Prince Ruprecht of Bavaria, one of Germany's most thoughtful and successful soldiers, noted in his diary that the capture of a French shell containing phials of supposedly poisonous gas was a 'welcome find' as 'our side' was intending to use the same. He told both Falkenhayn and Dr Haber that he found the new weapon personally distasteful, and also reminded his guests that the Western Allies would certainly deploy their industrial strength to provide gas to use against Germany, and that when they did they would have the prevailing westerly winds entirely in their favour. He thought the Allies would have a tenfold advantage in this respect. Haber doubted that the enemy's chemical industry could produce sufficient gas to win the advantage. Ruprecht, like de Tocqueville before him, warned that once a democracy is goaded into a course of action, it sees it through implacably. The Germans seem to have concluded that the productive capacity of their chemical industry would outweigh the iron laws of geography and meteorology.

The commander of Fourth German Army, Duke Albrecht of Württemberg, on whose front the attack would be made, was considering various plans to attack the Salient and capture Ypres. He was encouraged in this by Falkenhayn, who had decided on a major offensive against the Russians in the east, and was looking to the Western Front commanders to provide diversionary attacks to keep the Allies busy while troops were moved eastwards. After considerable labour, 6,000 gas cylinders were in place on the southern face of the Salient, but the necessary wind would not come. Duke Albrecht selected a new attack zone, on the northern front opposite Langemarck. The delays were worrying to the German High Command, who daily feared that their secret might be discovered. Indeed, there were an extraordinary number of warnings accumulating, but none of them seemed to register the scale of the impending danger.

April 1915: Warnings no Gentleman Could Believe

One report suggests that a British trench raid near Zillebeke on 28 March captured a German officer who revealed the plan for a gas attack, and that a subsequent patrol found the gas cylinders in place. This story would only surface in the British press eighteen years later. The French Tenth Army also reported that captured prisoners explained about the gas cylinders and the special pioneers, whom they called 'Stinkpionier', trained to release gas clouds. As the French were just then handing their trenches over to British troops, the report was 'lost' in the system. On 9 April *The Times* carried a short report headed: 'A New German Weapon: Poisonous gas for our troops.' It included the warning garnered from prisoners of war: 'They propose to asphyxiate our men if they advance by means of poisonous gas. The gas is contained under pressure in steel cylinders, and, being of a heavy nature, will spread along the ground without being dissipated quickly.'

Background

As the report spoke largely of fighting in the Argonne region, it was not much remarked upon in Flanders.

Meanwhile the Germans proceeded with their preparations for the attack. On 8 April their Fourth Army made it quite clear that the attackers were only to seize a line marked by the road connecting Boesinghe, Pilckem, Langemarck and Poelcappelle. This crossed a slight elevation that would become infamous as Mauser Ridge. Though it hardly deserved the name 'ridge', it was a piece of relatively high ground that opened onto a smooth slope over which enemy counter-attacks would have to cross. It would dominate a perfect 'killing field'. The German orders specified: 'After the objective is reached the troops are at once to dig in, arranging for mutual flanking support by means of strongpoints.' Two days later the Chief of Staff of Fourth Army, Major General Ilse, met with Falkenhayn to discuss the operation. Falkenhayn was simultaneously keen for the attack to go ahead as an experiment and pessimistic about its chances of success. When asked to provide an extra division to exploit any success towards Ypres he flatly refused, and even threatened to remove some of the troops already under orders to make the attack. He was much more interested in the upcoming offensive on the Eastern Front and saw the gas experiment purely as a diversionary measure. Fourth Army began to shift some of its own divisions around to provide something of a local reserve. 43rd Reserve Infantry Division (XXII Reserve Corps) came down from the Yser Canal to Roulers, and the Guards Cavalry Division moved to Bruges.

The gas cylinders, organised in batteries of twenty, were in place by 11 April, and the troops in their vicinity were issued with a cotton waste pad that covered the mouth and nose which, when soaked in a solution that was 30 per cent sodium sulphate, would protect against the effects of chlorine gas. After the several general and vague references to a gas attack had failed to convince anyone of imminent danger, on 13 April a German deserter brought a much more specific warning. Private August Jaeger, 234th Reserve Infantry Regiment (51st Reserve Division), had been an officer's chauffeur but had been returned to 'C' Company in the trenches. Disgruntled, he crossed over into the arms of the French 4th Chasseurs (11th 'Iron' Division). Besides giving hugely valuable intelligence on German trench routines, artillery and rest camp locations, and even the very house where his regimental commander was domiciled in Poelcappelle, he went on to give the most detailed description of the planned gas attack, the signals that would be fired to announce it, and the masks issued to the German infantry. The French divisional commander, Edmond Ferry, took this seriously. Besides ordering his own troops to thin out their ranks in the front-line trenches to reduce casualties in any such attack, this excellent soldier sent warnings to the British 28th Division on his right, and to the two Canadian brigades that were scheduled to start relieving 11th Division in the line on 14 April. He also informed his corps commander, Balfourier, and Henri Putz, the French Army commander. It would seem that Putz was the first to openly discount the story, suggesting that Jaeger was planted to spread disinformation. Nevertheless he saw that the news was passed to the King of the Belgians, to General Foch at Cassel and to French General Headquarters.

Campaign Chronicle

➤◆◅

15 April: Changing Winds

The Germans hoped the attack could be delivered on 15 April. While XXVI Reserve Corps was still assigned to capture the line Boesinghe–Poelcappelle, the revised orders suggested that achieving this might make the whole Ypres Salient untenable for the Allies. Now XXIII Reserve Corps was added to the attack plan, to assault the line of the Ypres canal from Steenstraat to Het Sas. During the night of 14/15 April the Germans made ready to attack, with infantry poised in the front-line trenches and reserves moving into place. The erstwhile favourable wind changed direction completely and the whole attack had to be stood down. That the predicted attack did not take place added to the scepticism amongst some Allied commanders about this 'impossible' idea, that civilised men would resort to poison gas.

One such decent man who must have heaved a sigh of relief when the threatened gas attack did not take place was Lieutenant General Sir Herbert Plumer, commander of British V Corps. He would achieve renown as the most careful of army commanders, earning the sobriquet 'Daddy' Plumer from the men who loved serving in his Second Army. He spent the day in discussions with his divisional commanders, Alderson (1st Canadian), Bulfin (28th) and Snow (27th), suggesting they put their medical services on a high state of alert but without direct reference to a possible gas attack. At the personal request of the commander of Second Army, General Sir Horace Smith-Dorrien, 6th Squadron, Royal Flying Corps flew aerial missions to photograph the enemy lines, looking for signs of reported batteries of cylinders. They were too well camouflaged and no unusual activity could be seen. Ironically, the fact that the Germans had not massed special reserves for an assault played to their advantage as no 'unusual' activity could be detected behind the lines, helping to convince Allied commanders that there was no attack impending. Smith-Dorrien wrote in his diary: 'One cannot take chances in a war like this, and in case there is any truth in it I have to let all commanders know.' It was this general warning that Plumer passed on to his divisional commanders 'for what it is worth'. The addition of this qualifying phrase is held up as an example of the short-sightedness of British generals but one is left wondering what exactly they were supposed to do at such short notice. The routine evening 'Stand To' was observed with special care and attention on 15 April but, again, it passed without incident. A second German deserter, Julius Rapsahl, 4th Ersatz Reserve Infantry Regiment (attached to 51st Reserve Infantry Division), had given much useful information but suggested that the gas masks they had been issued were a defensive measure against Allied use of gas.

Next day the French High Command told General Ferry that 'all this gas business cannot be taken seriously' and, for good measure,

Sir Horace Smith-Dorrien (1858–1930)

Born in 1858, Smith-Dorrien attended Harrow School and went to Sandhurst in 1876. He was commissioned into the Derbyshire Regiment and was on a staff assignment when he became one of the very few British survivors of the massacre of a British column by the Zulus at the Battle of Isandlwana in 1879. He served in Egypt 1882–1887, passed through Staff College 1887–1889, served in India 1890–1898 and was at the Battle of Omdurman in 1898. He had an excellent combat record during the Boer War, returning to India from 1901–07. He commanded at Aldershot 1907–1912 after Sir John French. His reforms there were so widely acclaimed that Sir John seems to have taken offence at the implied criticism of his tenure. From 1912–1914 Smith-Dorrien was at Southern Command and, when Sir James Grierson died in August 1914, he was appointed by Kitchener to command II Corps. He was not

Sir John French's preferred choice.

Smith-Dorrien was in the thick of the fighting at Mons, Le Cateau, the Marne and Aisne, and First Ypres. He incurred the undying wrath of French for his disobedient but necessary stand to fend off the dangerously close pursuit of the Germans at Le Cateau. In December 1914 he became the first commander of Second Army. In a letter to his wife, written on 13 March 1915, he described his relationship with French: 'Sir John is furious – not that that is unusual, for he appears now to live in a state of unreasonable fury. I don't mind, but it would make things easier if one had not such a wild beast to deal with.' Smith-Dorrien presided over the opening battles of Second Ypres and his wholly reasonable suggestion of falling back to stronger positions was taken by French as the opportunity to first remove most of his troops from his command, and finally to dismiss him.

Smith-Dorrien should have taken command of British forces in East Africa but was prevented from doing so by illness. He was Governor of Gibraltar 1918–1923, after which he retired from the Army. In 1925 he published *Memories of Forty-Eight Years' Service*, in which he was remarkably restrained about his relations with Sir John French, at whose funeral he served as a pallbearer. He appeared in the 1926 film 'Mons' as himself. Smith-Dorrien died from injuries sustained in a car accident in 1930.

He was a real soldier's soldier, with an outstanding combat record. His infamous outbursts of temper are now thought to be undiagnosed neuralgia. He was loyal to his Chief in the BEF and would not be drawn into the ensuing controversy.

censured him for speaking to his British allies directly without going through the proper channels, and for thinning out the troops in his front line without first gaining permission to do so. Ferry felt he had done all he could to alert the Allies to the danger and, besides, his division was pulled out to join the spring offensive to the south. (In a curious sequel to his part in the story, General Ferry named the deserter, Jaeger, in a 1932 article, whereupon the wretched man was arrested in Weimar Germany. Convicted of desertion and betrayal by the Reich's Supreme Court, Jaeger was sentenced to ten years' imprisonment in December 1932 – a grim prospect, given that the Nazis came to power the following year.)

By chance the very day that some French generals dismissed the threat, 16 April, Belgian intelligence forwarded the news that the Germans had placed a huge order for gas masks with a Belgian factory. What would have alarmed the Allies even more if they had been aware of it was the sharp increase in German reports of gas weapons being used against them. They claimed the French had used gas shells and bombs on 13, 14 and 16 April, and that the British had lent artillery support to a gas attack on the lines east of Ypres on 17 April. These stories were fed to the German troops to good effect. In post-war writings German soldiers told how they were fired up by this propaganda and were keen to volunteer to make 'revenge' attacks on the French and British. It would be many years before the Germans apologised for this blatant lie.

17 April: The Battle for Hill 60

Concerns about whether or not the Germans were going to use gas in the near future were soon subsumed in the savage fighting that erupted around Hill 60, south-east of Ypres. Any high ground assumed great importance in the generally flat country around Ypres. Hill 60, not a natural hill but a spoil heap from the nearby railway cutting, gave excellent views all the way to the city centre. It had been wrested from the French by the Germans in December 1914, and now the British decided they wanted it back. The attack by 13th Brigade, 5th Division, was rehearsed between 10 and 15 April. In an early experiment in the techniques of siege warfare that would reach full maturity at the Battle of Messines in June 1917, Welsh miners drove seven mines under Hill 60. These were detonated in three explosions at ten-second intervals, followed by an intense fifteen-minute artillery bombardment. A DCLI witness wrote, 'Clods of earth and debris of all kinds (including mangled Germans) shot up into the air'. Well-trained storming parties of 1st Royal West Kents cleared the fifty or so dazed German survivors of a company of 172nd Infantry Regiment off the hill in a matter of minutes. For only seven casualties, they captured fifty-three Germans, including four officers. Two companies of 2nd King's

Own Scottish Borderers, together with Royal Engineers, followed closely acting as pioneers and carrying material and ammunition up to consolidate the position. All the attackers thought the Germans had fled the hill rather precipitately, and then noticed the curious large cylinders lying about in disarray in the captured trenches. The British mine explosions and artillery fire had smashed up those batteries of gas cylinders that had been placed for the original intended attack on the south-east face of the Salient. The surviving German defenders were understandably anxious to flee the scene before the cylinders were ruptured. That night they hurled such verbal abuse at the British that the witness could not possibly set down their remarks in print!

In several days of vicious fighting Hill 60 would gain an evil reputation for the troops of both sides. Early on 18 April, from about 1 am, the Germans began counter-attacking the lost position. Estimates vary at between forty-four and fifty German artillery batteries subjecting the hill to intense bombardment. Having relieved the Royal West Kents in the front trenches, the KOSB were themselves in urgent need of relief by the Duke of Wellington's by 11.30 am, having lost ten officers and 210 other ranks in a few hours' fighting. By 3 pm the Duke's and 2nd King's Own Yorkshire Light Infantry were ordered to retake the lost portions of Hill 60. They both filed up along communication trenches and massed about 80 yards from the foot of the hill. With two companies in the assault, one following on with extra spades and hand grenades, and one in reserve, the two battalions stormed back over the hill at 6 pm. Losses were heavy but they set to work immediately to repair and improve the defences, under heavy enemy artillery fire. Another furious counter-attack was driven off, during which the men fired their rifles until the heat generated caused them to jam. As their own ammunition ran low, the men seized the large quantities of German rifles and ammunition lying about and used them effectively against their former owners. 'A Belgian artillery officer who witnessed the fighting said that both sides paid no attention to cover and shot at one another standing in the open.'

On 19 April 15th Brigade began to relieve a played-out 13th Brigade on the tortured hill: 1st Bedfords took over the front line and, when a quick counter-attack got into their trenches, they called on 9th Londons (Queen Victoria's Rifles, TF) to quickly evict them. 1st East Surreys were kept busy trying to repair the damaged trenches under a relentless bombardment. At 3 pm on 20 April, after heavy shelling, the Germans burst out of an advanced sap. The courage of the East Surrey private, Edward Dwyer, held them up long enough for the battalion to beat off the attack. Dwyer was awarded the Victoria Cross. At 4 pm the battalion headquarters was heavily shelled and the CO, Major Patterson, was killed. The front trenches collapsed yet again and, within the hour, German infantry assaulted from the railway cutting near the Caterpillar (another spoil heap nearby) towards the large crater on the right. The machine guns of the East Surreys, the rifles of 1st Norfolks and the Royal Artillery defeated this attack. Two Victoria Crosses were awarded to officers of 1st East Surreys. Second Lieutenant Geary inspired the defence of the left crater all through the night of 20/21 April. Lieutenant Roupell, though wounded in several places, refused to quit his post and crossed shell-swept ground to guide in the reinforcements. In the front line the men found the new, long-handled British hand grenade rather difficult to wield in such narrow trenches, so they resorted to the dangerous practice of grabbing incoming German grenades and throwing them back before they exploded. The Bedfords came up to reinforce the line, and the Queen Victoria's Rifles were near at hand. Though supposedly serving as carrying parties, the Queen Victoria's often found themselves engaged in front-line fighting. Second Lieutenant Woolley, 'the only officer on the hill at the time', assumed command of a leaderless group of some thirty men in a particularly sharp fight and won the first Victoria Cross awarded to a member of the Territorial Force. Finally the telephone wires were repaired and forward observation officers were able to direct artillery fire to break up the enemy attacks before they left their packed trenches. The craters and mangled trenches were choked with dead and wounded but, once again, the defenders of Hill 60 had hung on by the slightest of margins.

The BEF is Back in the Salient

Back in the Salient proper the British V Corps completed its relief of the French divisions around some two-thirds of the perimeter (a 10-mile frontage), so that the French could build up a reserve for their forthcoming spring offensive. The 27th Division had taken over the right from 2 April, 28th Division the centre from 8 April, and 1st Canadian Division came in on the left by 17 April. Next to them was the French 45th (Algerian) Division, and 87th Territorial Division, manning some 5 miles of the front. Beyond that troops of the Belgian Army were entrenched behind the Canal. As in every trench relief between the two nations throughout the war there were vociferous and protracted complaints from the British about the disgusting condition of the French trenches they took over. The French staff and regimental officers were perfectly correct in their handover of the lines, but the trenches themselves defied description. Open latrines, where they existed at all, dead bodies incorporated in the parapets or thinly covered in the floors, and a general absence of any kind of sanitation made them filthy and noisome. While the wire was often well placed, the trenches were of indifferent and inconsistent quality. The French depended far more on the rapid fire of their 75mm field guns to defend their front positions and were not too bothered about trenches and dug-outs. One Canadian engineer officer will suffice as witness: 'They [the trenches] were in a deplorable state and in a very filthy condition, all the little broken down side trenches and shell holes apparently being used as latrines and burial places for bodies.'

The other curiosity that often greeted British troops taking over French sectors of the line was the 'Live and Let Live' arrangements the French often had with opposing German units. This phenomenon, where troops in close proximity find ways to avoid fighting each other on a daily and wearisome basis, was more widely practised in the Great War than might be realised. But if it became too blatant, some regiments felt honour-bound to remind the enemy that there was a war on. Thus when 3rd Monmouths relieved the French in Polygon Wood they were affronted to see German troops moving about in the open and even cooking their breakfast sitting on the parapet. A few volleys of rifle fire cleared the enemy away. Inevitably there was retaliation – by hand grenade and trench mortar – for this violation of 'trench etiquette'. As a result the tour of duty, 8–12 April, proved more costly than usual.

The British and Canadian troops began at once to improve the strength and sanitary state of the lines. Fortunately the French had begun a much better defence line, running from Zillebeke Lake in the south to just east of Wieltje, where it bent back and ran towards the canal at Boesinghe. This 'GHQ Line', as it was known, was not continuous yet, but had excellent wire entanglements along most of its length, and if some of the trenches existed only in outline, it was lined with well-built strongpoints, with interlocking fields of fire.

19 April: Another False Start

The Germans hoped that the weather conditions would be right on 19 April and, once again, their troops assembled for the assault during the previous particularly dark night. When the wind failed to materialise in the morning the Germans had to disperse all the forward troops and guns as quickly as possible, before the Allies noticed these odd movements. They were greatly aided by a thick morning mist – so common in the spring and autumn in Flanders. The mist concealed a monumental traffic jam as the troops and their equipment tried to squeeze back into the cover provided by Houthoulst Forest.

The Germans had brought ninety-two heavy howitzers up to Ypres, including the colossal 42cm Krupps howitzer. Known to German soldiers as 'Dicke Bertha' (after Krupps' wife), it is well-known in English as 'Big Bertha'. It started lobbing its 1-ton shells into Ypres, at the rate of ten an hour, as part of a massive bombardment plan to distract the Allies from anything happening in the front lines. On 20 April one of its shells struck the headquarters of 82nd Brigade and, of those present, only one captain of the Rifle Brigade emerged alive.

The British Town Major who had administrative control of Ypres recorded the destruction in his diary, with nine civilians killed almost every day and many more wounded. Soon no civilians were allowed into Ypres and those living there – still nearly 2,000 in number – were being encouraged to leave. The centre of the town was systematically flattened, including the iconic Cloth Hall and St Martin's Cathedral.

On 21 April Falkenhayn visited Duke Albrecht at Fourth Army Headquarters to urge upon him the importance of creating a major diversion on the Western Front to assist operations in the East. As luck would have it the Army's meteorologists had given the very next day as a good opportunity to release the gas cloud. That day the DCLI captured a prisoner at Hill 60 who confidently 'stated that the Germans would be in Ypres by the 22nd'.

22–23 April: The Battle of Gravenstafel Ridge

The First Shock

At midnight on 21/22 April the German infantry had been told the attack would definitely take place at some time on the 22nd – codename 'Gott strafe England'. They made sure their gas masks were ready, and cleared gaps in their own wire leading out into No Man's Land. The pioneers removed sandbags from in front of the batteries of gas cylinders. The first attack time, 5.45 am, came and went with no sign of the necessary wind behind them. In the packed forward trenches the infantry and gas pioneers had to wait in nervous anticipation. The next message said that it would be at least 4 pm before the attack could go ahead. They were told that the signal for the release of gas would be a red flare fired from a balloon over Houthoulst Forest, and a single shell fired from 'Big Bertha' into Ypres. Until then everything had to be kept very quiet, to avoid provoking artillery fire from the other side.

Thursday, 22 April, was a glorious spring day in the Salient – sunny and warm. The ground was drying; green shoots and spring flowers were adding colour to the shell-ploughed fields. At 3 pm 3rd Canadian Brigade received a message from Division that 100 mouth-organs for the entertainment of the troops were available for collection at their convenience. Pilots of the Royal Flying Corps noted that the Germans seemed quite 'busy' in their back areas but the front was relatively quiet. The fact that the Germans had not brought extra troops and artillery into the area – usually a sure sign of impending attack – was working to their advantage. The relentless shelling of the town of Ypres intensified noticeably in the afternoon. The French artillery, with their inimitable 75mm guns, began a furious response to the increased German artillery fire. Canadian soldiers in various parts of the Salient – officers riding along the canal, forward observers of the artillery, men of 3rd Brigade in the front line – reported soon after 5 pm 'a queer sky' or, more specifically, 'a cloud of peculiar colour (greyish, yellowish, greenish), darker near the ground and lighter in colour near the top'. Some British officers, even Smith-Dorrien himself (returning from a pep talk to the men just relieved at Hill 60) noticed a 'peculiar smell' in the air. Several observers noted how the French rifle fire burst into activity but gradually died away. The gas cloud looked for a time as if it might engulf the Canadian front trenches, but it veered away to the left and struck the French line everywhere.

The Germans released 180,000 kilos (168 tons) of chlorine gas on a 6-kilometre front, from 1,600 of the original large cylinders and 4,130 of the half-cylinders. The discharge took five minutes to complete. The two French divisions in the line saw two 'yellowish green clouds' appear either side of Langemarck at 5 pm. Beyond that village the two clouds merged into one and soon the unprotected infantry were weeping and gasping as the chlorine took effect. There was a brave effort to fire into the approaching clouds, and the French artillery poured out their stream of shells in defensive fire. At 5.10 pm the German artillery delivered a concentrated deluge of fire onto the French positions for ten minutes. Then the German infantry, wearing masks, climbed out of their trenches and followed the gas cloud as it drifted on a light breeze over the enemy lines. As the gas thickened over their positions, most of the two French divisions fled in a blind panic to the rear: 'They turned and as quickly as their tortured bodies would allow poured back down the roads leading to Ypres. None could blame them.' Eyewitnesses all convey the horror of watching unprotected men gasping, retching, choking, and dying before them. Civilians were caught up in the gas cloud and added to the scenes of torment as they fled back to the canal. French reserves waiting there caught just enough of the thinning gas cloud, and saw the terrified fugitives, and many of them took flight.

'Everyone is Dying Around Me'

The German infantry had been taught no special tactics to carry out the attack; it was too novel an experience for any 'doctrine' to have developed. Speed was of the essence to achieve the strictly limited objectives on the day. They were simply told to advance with bayonets fixed and with rifles unloaded. We know the latter instruction was largely ignored as the French infantry reported being fired on as they retreated. When the French guns fell silent around 7 pm everyone knew there was serious trouble in the

Salient. The Germans had captured some 2,000 prisoners and fifty-one guns, including sixteen French 75mm field guns and twenty-nine old but powerful 90mm guns, and a battery of four British heavy pieces taken in Kitchener's Wood. The Germans were able to turn the fire of some of the captured French guns on the Canadians. French casualties for this terrible day are hard to compute but may have been as high as 6,000 killed, wounded and gassed, all within a couple of hours. Officers of 1st Tirailleurs managed to telephone back a warning of the catastrophe. Commandant Fabry reported: 'Everyone is dying around me . . . I am abandoning my command post.' French Territorials could be seen staggering back carrying boxes and long poles. They were saving their regimental trophies and colours.

All British observers of these awful events agreed that no men could be expected to withstand the shock of the first use of this gas weapon. The official position was expressed by Sir John French in the *London Gazette* (10 July 1915):

> I wish particularly to repudiate any idea of attaching the least blame to the French division [*sic* – there were two involved] for this unfortunate incident. After all the examples our gallant Allies have shown of dogged and tenacious courage in the many trying situations in which they have been placed throughout the course of this campaign it is quite superfluous for me to dwell on this aspect of the incident, and I would only express my conviction that, if any troops in the world had been able to hold their trenches in the face of such a treacherous and altogether unexpected onslaught, the French Division would have stood firm.

Within half an hour the German 52nd Reserve Infantry Division had gained its objective, the Pilckem Ridge. According to their instructions, they immediately began to dig in and consolidate their success at around 6 pm. This was a blessing in disguise for the Allies, for there was precious little to prevent the Germans driving into Ypres itself. Any German reserves that might conceivably have been used to exploit success (two Landwehr and one Ersatz Reserve brigades) had been drawn into the line to fill a gap that opened between XXIII and XXVI Reserve Corps. There was only one brigade of marine infantry left in reserve. Well might von Falkenhayn later opine, 'The surprise effect was very great. Unfortunately we were not in the position to exploit it to the full. The necessary reserves were not ready.' British observers suggested that, with five army corps and five brigades to hand, lack of numbers for Germany was not really the issue. If that were really so, why persist with the attacks for a month? After the war Haber would suggest that insufficient gas had been released in one attack, and that the soldiers lacked imagination. Basil Liddell Hart, a historian well-versed in universal military history, made a shrewd observation that took in the psychology of men in battle: 'But if lack of reserves was the fundamental cause of the Germans' failure, the immediate cause was the troops' fear of their own gas.' Having seen the appalling effect of chlorine gas on the French before them, and encountering pockets of gas lingering in hollows, they were only too willing to dig in at dusk and await further events.

The 51st Reserve Infantry Division had to fight its way through Langemarck, where the gas cloud had thinned considerably, and push on towards the line of the Steenbeek. Some German soldiers, wearing only rudimentary gas masks, said they were delayed by detouring around the gas pockets referred to above. About 6 pm they were ordered to push on in a south-easterly direction and made crossings of the Steenbeek at two places some 1,300 yards south-west of Poelcappelle. The stiffening resistance of the Canadians prevented any further progress towards St Julien.

Gallant Little Belgium

The 45th and 46th Reserve Infantry Divisions advanced to the line of the Yser Canal. But the gas had largely dissipated itself on this sector, and 2nd *bis* Zouaves and 7th Zouaves rallied and, together with some French gunners and Territorials, put up a spirited resistance at the bridges at Boesinghe. As the French barricaded the bridges the Germans were obliged to dig in after several failed assaults. The Belgians put up a tremendous fight that held the enemy infantry up until the late evening. The French 87th Division sent its 80th Regiment towards Steenstraat, but it was pinned down by machine-gun fire. Its sister regiment, the 76th, came up to Het Sas and tried to stabilise the line there. Later that night at two places, Steenstraat and the Het Sas lock (just south of Lizerne), the German 211th and 212th Reserve Infantry Regiments crossed the canal and set up bridgeheads on the western bank. The Belgian Grenadiers kept the line intact at Steenstraat, and were joined in the nick of time by 2nd Carabiniers. Belgian artillery fired in support of the French, and 6th Division formed a flank guard that sealed off the left-hand side of the German advance. Some time after 7.30 pm German artillery hit them with gas shells and a determined frontal assault of the canal line was launched. Not one boat or raft even reached the water as the Belgian infantry and artillery shot the attack to pieces. It was a very fine defensive success, for which they do not get enough credit.

A Swift Response to the Emergency

The commanders of the front-line troops on the other flank of the attack reacted swiftly and decisively. Brigadier General Turner, 3rd Canadian Brigade, ordered St Julien to be put in a state of defence, and ordered his reserve battalion (14th Canadian Infantry) up to Mouse Trap Farm, then serving as brigade headquarters. They found elements of 1/1st Tirailleurs and 1/2nd *bis* Zouaves gamely holding their positions on their immediate left. The Canadian field artillery began immediately to fire in support of the French. One artillery officer said he heard more shells fired in one hour than he had witnessed in the whole of his service in the Boer War. Probing attacks towards Mouse Trap Farm were defeated by 13th Canadian Infantry, with help from a company of the 14th and two guns of 10th Battery. The first Victoria Cross of the battle was awarded to Lance Corporal Frederick Fisher, 13th Battalion, for keeping his Colt machine gun in action after its crew had become casualties, and fighting on until he was killed whilst covering the withdrawal of 10th Canadian Field Battery.

As news of the attack reached divisional headquarters, Alderson placed his reserve battalion, 16th Canadian Scottish, at Turner's disposal and called up 10th Canadian Infantry from its labouring duties in the rear. The 2nd Canadian Brigade had already ordered its reserve battalion, the 7th, to be ready to move west if needed.

Second Army Headquarters (at Hazebrouck) received news of the attack via V Corps (Poperinghe) at about 6.45 pm. Within the hour they knew the full story of the French collapse and of the Canadians' swift response to the threat. General Putz had to admit that a 3,000-yard gap had opened up in the front line. Smith-Dorrien gave 1st Cavalry Brigade to V Corps and by 8.15 pm Plumer had sent 2nd and 3rd Canadian Infantry Battalions and 2nd East Yorkshires (from 28th Division's reserve) to Alderson. By 8.25 pm Alderson was able to reassure the High Command that his line was secure, and that a flank guard had been thrown back to cover one side of the German penetration of the line. Mouse Trap Farm was a secure hinge on which the defence was based. French infantry (elements of 7th Zouaves) were reported moving into the GHQ Line to cover Ypres. After a brief rest from the fighting at Hill 60, 13th Brigade was on its way back to that dismal place when, near Ypres, they were halted by the stream of refugees. They were soon allocated to Alderson's 1st Canadian Division and went into reserve at Brielen, on the canal, to await further orders.

Sir Herbert Plumer (1857–1932)

Born in 1857, Plumer was commissioned into the York and Lancaster Regiment, serving with them in India, Aden, and the Sudan. He passed Staff College 1885–1887, coming nineteenth out of twenty-six candidates. He had long service in South Africa, including the Boer War. In 1902 he commanded 4th Infantry Brigade, was on the Army Council, and then commanded 5th Division from 1906. He was Sir John French's first choice for II Corps but didn't come out to the Western Front until December 1914 when he got command of the new V Corps.

During the fighting at Second Ypres Plumer was given command of Second Army when Smith-Dorrien was dismissed. He was immediately allowed to carry out the phased withdrawal that his former Chief had suggested. For the rest of the war, with an interlude in Italy from November 1917 to March 1918, Plumer commanded Second Army in the Salient. He conducted the Battle of Messines in June 1917, a classic set-piece application of siege warfare techniques in modern war. His careful 'bite and hold' operations during Third Ypres put the German Army under intolerable pressure until atrocious weather brought things to a close. His guardianship of the Salient contributed to the final victory in 1918.

Plumer commanded the British army of occupation in Germany 1918–1919, was Governor of Malta 1919–1924 and High Commissioner of Palestine 1925–1928. In 1927 he was the obvious choice to open the Menin Gate memorial to the missing.

Probably the best British Army Commander on the Western Front, Plumer was adored by the troops he led. To them he was 'Daddy' Plumer, in recognition of the care he took of them in and out of battle. He was fortunate in his excellent Chief of Staff, 'Tim' Harington. He was occasionally threatened by Sir Douglas Haig, who might well have been a little jealous of this enormously popular and capable soldier. In personal appearance he was the very model of 'Colonel Blimp'; in his character, quite the opposite.

In addition to the Canadian response, the commanders of 28th and 27th British Divisions (Bulfin and Snow) had already begun emergency measures without waiting for any instruction from above. 27th Division sent 4th Rifle Brigade towards St Jean, got 2nd Wessex Company, Royal Engineers, to put Wieltje in a high state of defence and brought 2nd King's Shropshire Light Infantry up from reserve to guard its divisional and brigade headquarters. 28th Division ordered 2nd Buffs and 3rd Middlesex to St Jean. The Buffs were shocked when 'machine-gun bullets came spattering into St Jean, which place ought to have been safe enough from this kind of fire.' Clearly the Germans were a lot closer than they ought to be. The 3rd Middlesex had, in fact, begun to move there under its own initiative on seeing the terrible flight of the gas-afflicted French infantry. The 5th King's Own were brought up in support, and 1st York and Lancasters were ordered forward from Ypres. These four battalions became the basis of 'Geddes Detachment', after their ad hoc commander, Colonel A. D. Geddes of the Buffs, and they passed under the immediate control of Alderson's Canadian Division. Major Power took over 2nd Buffs while his colonel acted as a local brigadier.

28th Division also released 2nd Cheshires and 1st Monmouths as a local reserve, which formed up under the shelter of Frezenburg Ridge.

At around 9 pm there was a gap in the front lines of some 8,000 yards. The right was firmly held by 3rd Canadian Brigade, with some French Tirailleurs doing what they could to assist. The left was secure behind the canal, strongly held by 6th Belgian Division. There were strongpoints at St Julien and Mouse Trap Farm, but they existed as islands in three gaps of 2,000, 1,000 and 3,000 yards respectively, the latter covered by a single French machine-gun crew.

After a slight pause, the local German commanders renewed their attacks to exploit the gap created. At 9 pm a sharp assault drove in 1/1st Tirailleurs, but about 200 of them rallied and, with six platoons of 13th Canadian Infantry, lined the Poelcappelle road and brought the enemy to a halt. The situation was still uncertain. It was thought sufficiently precarious to order the Canadian field artillery to pull back to less exposed positions. Mercifully the Germans seem to have also concluded that they could not achieve much more this late in the day and the fighting died down. While this attack had a limited objective, and was never intended as a 'breakthrough battle', it surprised the German commanders with the speed with which it succeeded and certainly opened up a remarkable opportunity to exploit the success. The lateness of the start of the attack, and the failure to supply sufficient reserves to reinforce the first wave of attackers, saved the Allies from a more serious defeat. Private McKenna of 16th Canadian Scottish spoke for many of the front-line soldiers when he later wrote, 'I cannot help thinking that the enemy lost a wonderful opportunity, for surely he could have walked through us like a man could walk through a hoop of paper'.

Between 9 and 10 pm Smith-Dorrien warned GHQ of the 'grave situation', and urged Sir John French to insist on French reinforcement as a matter of urgency. Foch, as pugnacious as ever, had already ordered General Putz to counter-attack immediately to recover the lost positions, and had ordered the newly-formed 153rd Division of Tenth Army up from Arras to his aid, with more divisions promised. All around the Salient troops in deep reserve (the British Cavalry Corps and 50th Division, which had arrived in France just three days before) were being ordered to prepare for movement. The Territorials from Northumbria were reasonably expecting to go into a quiet part of the line to learn the routine of trench warfare. Theirs was to be a more immediate baptism of fire.

Counter-Attack at Once!

Foch's obsession with the attack was to have tragic consequences. He ordered Putz to retake Pilckem at about 8 pm. Putz immediately requested assistance from the British. Alderson ordered 3rd Canadian Brigade to retake Kitchener's Wood, to aid the French effort and to recover the four 4.7-inch heavy guns of 2nd London Heavy Battery that had been lost there in the first German attack. The wood, on the eastern end of Mauser Ridge, overlooked St Julien and Mouse Trap Farm, and it was not advisable to let the enemy get too well established there undisturbed. Behind Mauser Ridge the Germans would be able to assemble, unobserved, to renew their assault the next day. It was 8.40 pm before the order reached brigade headquarters, and it would be some hours before the troops could be assembled and instructed for the attack. The 10th Canadian Infantry (later famous as the Calgary Highlanders) – not actually part of 3rd Brigade but they arrived on the scene first – were to make the attack, closely supported by the 16th (Canadian Scottish). It is accepted military wisdom that an immediate counter-attack, carried out with rapidity, determination and courage, can often, or even invariably, 'bounce' an enemy out of a newly won position before he has time to consolidate. But on this occasion the French counter-attack – supposedly the main effort, to which two Canadian and a Belgian battalion were to lend help – simply failed to materialise. The Canadian infantry unknowingly went in alone in their first serious attack of the war.

Kitchener's Wood

At 10.47 pm 3rd Canadian Brigade, with little knowledge of the enemy strength or dispositions, issued its final orders for the attack at 11.30 pm. It was a bitterly cold night. The 9th and 12th Canadian Batteries and one British field battery would provide fire support. The often-practised formation was selected, of an attack on a two-company frontage (some 300 yards), with three further waves each of two companies following at 30-yard intervals. The 10th Battalion, 816 strong, formed their companies in two ranks;

the kilted Canadian Scottish formed up behind them. Some 100 bombers drawn from 2nd and 3rd Canadian Brigades were added to the attack. The men were 'very quiet, but keen. Discipline was perfect'. Colonel Boyle of the 10th, much admired by his men, told them: 'We have been aching for a fight, and now we are going to get it.' A chaplain moved amongst the men telling them, 'It's a great day for Canada.'

The officers of both attacking battalions met to synchronise watches and discuss the attack. It was feared that Oblong Farm, off to the left, would be a problem. Machine guns there would enfilade the attackers, but it did not figure in their orders and had to be ignored. The attack could not begin until the Canadian Scottish was all assembled, and that was not until 11.45 pm. At 11.48, to whispered orders, some 1,500 men advanced with their rifles at the high port. They had some 500 yards to cover in a failing moonlight and the first half was covered quickly and silently, with the lines going 'steadily ahead, as if they were doing a drill manoeuvre'. With some 200 yards to go they ran into the line of a thick hedge, threaded with barbed wire. Though there was no talking in the ranks, the noise caused by getting through the obstacle alerted the enemy. As 10th Battalion reformed beyond the hedge a German flare soared skywards and a storm of fire burst out from front and flank. One sergeant recalled the bullets sounding like 'a hailstorm on a zinc roof'. Despite heavy losses, the two battalions, now thoroughly mixed up, charged home. Private McKenna described the attack: 'In order to deceive the enemy in regard to our numbers, we were told to make as much noise as we could and the shouting, swearing, cursing at the top of our voices was terrific!' The German trench along the southern edge of the wood was quite shallow and it took less than a minute to storm it and push on into the wood. All four company commanders of the 10th had fallen, and there was some real hand-to-hand fighting in the dark wood, a relatively rare occurrence in this war. Some French troops had joined the attack and, as they headed north-east towards their old front line, the Canadians tended to follow them and veered away to the right. By midnight the wood was taken, with only minimal artillery support and partial surprise. Apparently large numbers of Germans were sufficiently surprised to offer their surrender, but the attackers were too few in number to accept them. The Canadians' fearsome reputation for taking few prisoners got an early boost. Those prisoners taken were largely from 234th Reserve Infantry Regiment (51st Reserve Division), including a colonel. The claim that prisoners were taken from 2nd Prussian Guards Regiment cannot be borne out by the German Order of Battle.

The 4.7-inch heavy guns of the London Battery were recovered but, with no means of removing them, they were instead smashed beyond any use to the enemy. The two battalions tried to consolidate their position but were under fire from three sides. Sergeant Hall, 10th Battalion, described 'a terrible concentration of shells sweeping the wood – it was just like a tropical storm sweeps a forest'. Gradually 10th Battalion assembled to defend the left side of the wood; 16th looked after the right. Some brave NCOs pushed ahead to locate the enemy lines but were caught in the open and had to dash back to safety. One German strongpoint held out in the south-west corner. The defenders, speaking excellent English, called on the Canadians to surrender. A hastily arranged frontal assault on the position was bloodily defeated. The survivors of the attack managed to dig a trench facing the enemy post. The officer leading the effort, Lieutenant Lowry, was badly wounded and sent back to report to brigade headquarters. Colonel

Marshal Ferdinand Foch (1851–1929)

Born in 1851 into a deeply Catholic family, a disadvantage in anti-clerical France at the time, Foch joined 4th Infantry Regiment in 1870, seeing active service in the Franco-Prussian War. He was commissioned into 24th Artillery in 1871. He attended Staff College in 1885 and was so brilliant there that he was its Instructor of Tactics from 1895. Hailed as 'the most original and subtle mind in the French Army', he wrote books on military history, focussing on the campaigns of the Napoleonic and Franco-Prussian wars. Famous for such pugnacious quotes as 'The will to conquer is the first condition of victory', he should not be confused with the blind cult of the offensive that gripped the French Army in the years before 1914.

In 1914 Foch commanded XX Corps in the Battles of the Frontiers, and then Ninth Army on the Marne. He played an important part at First Ypres as liaison between the French and British armies. In 1915 his role at Second Ypres must be considered a negative one, responsible through his moral ascendancy over Sir John French for the many wasteful and hopeless counter-attacks early in the battle. He conducted the costly Artois offensive, and in 1916 was an army group commander on the Somme. He was removed from active command by Joffre. In 1917 Foch was Chief of the French General Staff.

His great achievement was in 1918 when, as Supreme Allied Commander on the Western Front, he coordinated the resistance to the German spring offensives and then the massive series of counter-offensives that secured victory. He was made a Marshal of France in 1918, and lobbied for a harsh peace after the war. After various advisory posts in the 1920s, he died in 1929 and is buried at Les Invalides, Paris.

Foch was short, pugnacious, restless and vigorous. He could galvanise men in dire circumstances, and, with the exception of Second Ypres, was a positive force for Allied victory.

Boyle (10th Battalion) was well forward organising the defence of the wood when he was hit and mortally wounded. His second-in-command, Major Maclaren, had already been wounded and together the two wounded officers made their way to the rear. Command of the 10th devolved to the somewhat inexperienced adjutant, Major Dan Ormand.

At about 2.30 am on 23 April, Colonel Leckie of 16th Battalion decided the position was untenable and ordered both battalions back to their original front line. Their main problem in the withdrawal was being fired on by their comrades who refused to believe they were Canadians. The high incidence of English-speaking Germans causing confusion in British ranks was playing itself out once again. Sydney Cox, of 10th Battalion, remembered, 'our own fellows wouldn't believe it was us, and they were shooting at us. You would holler at them, and, "Oh, we've heard that, you can't fool us." Hardest time [sic] trying to convince our own fellows that we were Canadians.' Finally they made it back to the relative safety of their old front line. At later roll calls 10th Battalion numbered five officers and 188 men (out of 816); 16th had five officers and 263 men (about a third of their attack strength). The Germans captured two officers and twenty-six men of 10th Battalion in the confused fighting in the wood. The battalion only had thirty-five men taken prisoner in the entire course of the Great War; twenty-eight of them in this, their first action. Sergeant Stevenson recalled:

> I could see that havoc had been wrought on our boys, for all around were the dead bodies of men who, a few hours before, had been singing Canada's national song. They died with it on their lips, but their memory will live for many a day and year to come. For they made a name for the Dominion that will live in history.

Smith-Dorrien credited the Canadian attack with stabilising the situation on the night of 22 April. (We know now that the Germans were digging in with no intention of pushing on that late in the day.) Foch thought it one of the finest acts of the whole war. It was a very gallant action, launched in obedience to higher commands, and with little in the way of reconnaissance or preparation. The brigade and the division concerned would subsequently become famous in military history for the careful organisation of their attacks, but at this early stage in the war every element of the BEF still had a great deal to learn.

Around midnight the Germans had attacked at points along the front of 27th and 28th Divisions. Fighting from very poor trenches, only recently taken over from the French, the British claimed to have bloodily repulsed these attacks but the Germans claim they were just to pin British reserves in place. At 2 am, 23 April, the Germans renewed their pressure on the Keerselare crossroads and Brigadier General Turner needed help from 2nd Brigade to keep them at bay. These trenches were held by British, French and Canadian troops fighting shoulder to shoulder. There was a great problem with broken cables making communications very difficult. 27th Division's headquarters became the report centre for the entire battle. Motor cars and runners were the chief means of delivering messages. It was an anxious night for the

Allied commanders, not knowing whether the German assault would be renewed in the morning.

Already the defenders had been given advice about how to cope with the new gas weapon. Initially any sort of wet cloth was to be kept over the nose and mouth. Ideally it should be soaked in bicarbonate of soda, but that was understandably in short supply. Given that ammonia went some way to mitigate the effects of the chlorine gas, it was realised that urine was a short-term substitute. Desperate times called for desperate measures. Canadian medical officers remembered from their hospital training that urea combines with chlorine to form dichlorourea, which neutralises the more toxic aspects of chlorine.

The sense of outrage felt by the defending troops at this 'new frightfulness' in war would become an influential factor in the stubbornness of the fighting. This impassioned section of the history of the Buffs, written many years later, conveys the point:

The Second Battle of Ypres has brought more obloquy and ill-fame to the German nation than even Marathon brought glory to the Athenians. It appears to have been well understood by scientific men that a noisome and poisonous gas could be carried down wind that no man could breathe its suffocating fumes and live for long, and further that he must die in agony. At the ineffectual conference at The Hague it had been arranged between the representatives of the several nations, including Germany, that the use of such a disgusting and brutal weapon should be barred between civilised enemies, and nobody thought any more about it, but the German beast is not a gentleman and he ruled that the brave old days when foeman fought with a chivalrous regard for his opponent were to cease, at any rate as far as the much-vaunted Fatherland was concerned, and so this battle that we are now to consider goes down in history as the first great combat in which unfair and blackguardly methods were adopted.

*

In the early morning light of 23 April figures were seen approaching the Canadian front line wearing French uniforms and calling out, 'Nous sommes les Français'. Canadian suspicions were confirmed by a French officer, as he stood conversing with two Canadian officers supervising some strongpoint construction. A heavy fire was opened on the intruders and another 'manifestation of German guile was frustrated'.

The 'Geddes Detachment' was ordered at dawn to start reaching out towards its left, in an effort to join up their line with the French. The French were a long way short of being able to respond as quickly as Foch wished. They had lost all their guns east of the canal in the debacle of 22 April. To help them Geddes was ordered to counter-attack and try to recover some of the lost ground. Struggling with a tiny ad hoc staff, Geddes tried to get his men ready to attack at dawn, about 4 am. Keeping one battalion (1st York and Lancasters) in reserve, he could put only $2^{1}/4$ battalions (three companies of 2nd Buffs; two companies 3rd Middlesex; 5th King's Own) into the attack.

Geddes Force to the Rescue

The Buffs, under Major Power, moved forward by short rushes over open ground west of Mouse Trap Farm. They were under severe machine-gun fire from Mauser Ridge the whole time, where the Germans had dug two trench lines on a rising slope. Looking to his right, Major Power could see three lines of trenches linking up to the GHQ Line sitting quite empty of defenders. They offered an inviting gap to any forward movement by the Germans. By a half turn to the right he got the Buffs into the first line of trenches, sealing the breach temporarily. They lost two officers and eighty men before they stabilised the line near Hampshire Farm. In the general confusion they found Canadian and French troops in the line to their left. Their sacrifice helped 3rd Canadian Brigade to secure the left of its line. The Middlesex pushed out towards the left and linked up with 1st Canadian Brigade, deploying near the canal to assist any French counter-attack. There is a description of the arrival of the Buffs given by A. T. Hunter in *Canada and the Great War*, which speaks wonderfully of the nature of the British infantry:

These Buffs . . . now proceeded to fit into the Canadian line as if they belonged to it. For it is one of the virtues of the true English regiments that they are not temperamental and do not require humouring when in strange company; but fit comfortably into any section of a fight like interchangeable parts in a standardised machine.

The counter-attack against Mauser Ridge was duly made by 4th Canadian Infantry and two companies of 3rd Middlesex, supported by just one Canadian field battery. There was not a Frenchman to be seen. They advanced under heavy fire for half a mile before being driven to ground some 600 or 700 yards short of the enemy line. Some men found themselves sheltering in a field of square-cut manure piles. It wasn't long before they realised that these odd constructs provided more of an aiming point for the German infantry than shelter for the attackers. As 4th Canadians wavered in the advance their English colonel, Arthur Birchall (Royal Fusiliers), stepped forward, conspicuously tall, wearing his 'British warm' and carrying a light cane, and 'with great calmness and cheerfulness, rallied his men, but at the moment he had succeeded he was shot dead, struck by three bullets simultaneously. He had twice been wounded, but insisted on continuing with his command'. At 7.15 am 1st Canadian Infantry came forward to extend the line to the left. The force struggled to dig in as best it could under heavy fire, including gas shells later in the morning. Losses mounted rapidly in the hopeless affair.

At least the gap in the line had been reduced to 1,200 yards. The French had gathered five and half battalions of Zouaves and were readying themselves for a counter-attack. But seventeen and a half Allied battalions (twelve Canadian and five and a half British) were facing forty-two battalions of Germans, and the handful of guns (equivalent to half a divisional artillery) were outnumbered five to one in field guns alone, with nothing to counter the German heavy artillery.

The 23rd of April was bright and clear, so the Royal Flying Corps was able to make flights of inspection over the enemy lines all day. The RFC airmen reported that there was no great movement of reserves in the German rear – only local forces seemed to be moving forward. At least the hopeless British attacks had kept the enemy in a defensive posture. The RFC observed his efforts at improving his newly acquired line. The real problem was that the enemy could fire into the rear of the Canadian positions, making resupply a great difficulty, and there was already talk of digging a new line across the base of the Salient.

We know that German Fourth Army had wanted to renew the attack at 9 am on 23 April, directing XXIII Reserve Corps towards Poperinghe and XXVI Reserve Corps, with its right anchored on the canal line, was to drive south into the heart of the Salient. The other corps in the line were to make local attacks to pin the British in place, before XXVII Reserve Corps joined the XXVI in its drive for Ypres. The prompt Allied counter-attacks, however doomed they seemed, were sufficient to completely disrupt German intentions all day. The Germans later complained that they lacked the necessary reserves to exploit their first-day success and the troops were not familiar enough with the terrain to risk attacks that had not been carefully prepared. Artillery fire from west of the canal caused serious loss to XXVI Reserve Corps.

Closing the Gap

By 9.30 am 1st Canadian Brigade and French lines finally met up and the gap was closed. The French were still a long way from being ready to counter-attack, claiming the want of artillery as the reason. The 13th Brigade (5th British Division), supposedly resting after its ordeal at Hill 60, was given to Plumer as a corps reserve, and two battalions of 27th Division (2nd Duke of Cornwall's Light Infantry and 9th Royal Scots) were handed over to Alderson. He passed them on to Colonel Geddes, bringing his 'Geddes Force' to seven battalions (but still lacking even the equivalent of a brigade headquarters). Colonel Tuson of the DCLI was made temporary commander of a composite brigade (2nd DCLI, 9th Royal Scots, 4th Rifle Brigade and two companies of King's Shropshire Light Infantry). Captain Dene had to take command of the DCLI. Artillery east of the canal remained in very short supply. As the day continued to be relatively quiet but for the shelling, Foch and Sir John French met to discuss restoring the situation. Foch demanded that the lost ground be recovered. Although the British Field Marshal outranked him, the dynamic Foch had complete moral authority over Sir John. His attacking style suited the British Commander-in-Chief, but even he made some caveats about the proposed action. French said he was prepared to support counter-attacks but, if they did not happen soon, he would consider falling back to a more defensible line, to Foch's dismay. Meanwhile he continued to direct reserves towards the Salient: 50th (Northumbrian) Division (TF) drew near during the day; 149th Brigade was at Brandhoek, just west of Ypres; 150th Brigade reached 28th Division at about 12.15 pm; 151st Brigade was held as a V Corps reserve. The Cavalry Corps, based at Poperinghe, released its 1st Division to Second Army to stiffen the left; the remainder of the Corps stood in Army reserve. Many units had well-earned rests interrupted, with hurried orders to head for the Salient. The London Rifle Brigade (5th Londons) were annoyed at having to abandon an elaborately planned sports day. The Queen's Own Oxfordshire Hussars were hurried out of camp without a scheduled meal, took three hours to move 3 miles on crowded roads, only to be kept waiting for hours before they could get their horses fed and watered. The Lahore Division and two brigades of 4th Division also began to move north towards Ypres.

It was still thought by GHQ that the enemy should be attacked before he had more time to consolidate his positions. As the KOSB history puts it, 'In those days marked deference was paid to the French theory of defence by immediate counter-attack'. At 2.40 pm Sir John French obliged Smith-Dorrien to order Plumer to make a general attack all along the line from Kitchener's Wood to the canal. Smith-Dorrien, a thoughtful infantry soldier, could have had few illusions about the result of such impromptu attacks, but his relationship with his chief, soured during the retreat from Mons the previous year, was so bad that he could only obey or face the most serious consequences. Both Smith-Dorrien and Plumer came up to Alderson's headquarters (1st Canadian Division) to oversee the event. But the executive control of the battle was handed down to Brigadier General O'Gowan of 13th Brigade, which fact was not notified to Colonel Geddes until forty-five minutes before the start of the attack. As a result the two components of the attack, 13th Brigade west of the Ypres–Pilckem Road, and four battalions of 'Geddes Force' east of it, operated quite independently of each other. The French were supposed to assist with elements of their 45th Division. The 3 pm attack was postponed until 4.15 as 13th Brigade struggled to get into the line on time. In a double tragedy the artillery supporting the attack was not informed of the changed time and fired off its barrage from 2.45 to 3 pm, thus alerting the enemy that 'something was up', and then was not given the new start time and so failed to open fire again until after the attack had begun.

'Never had any Prospect of Success'

In sombre words the British Official History states simply: 'The attack to which the Second Army was committed by GHQ order at the request of the French never had any prospect of success.' It goes on to point out that eight British battalions were about to assail four brigades (twenty-four battalions) of entrenched Germans.

On the right Geddes led forward 2nd Duke of Cornwall's Light Infantry (27th Division), with two companies of 9th Royal Scots in support, and 2nd East Yorkshires and 1st York and Lancasters, supported by 5th King's Own (all from 28th Division); on the left 13th Brigade comprised 2nd King's Own Scottish Borderers and 1st Royal West Kents in the first line, with 2nd King's Own Yorkshire Light Infantry and 9th Londons (Queen Victoria's Rifles) in support. The 13th Brigade was described as 'well-fed, if weary' and its soldiers 'went in cheerfully'.

As the DCLI went forward, in the standard formation of two companies forward and two following:

> a coloured French soldier, unarmed and with his head tied up, came up and asked, in broken French, where we were going. On being told that we were about to attack he asked if he might accompany us. He was given a rifle and bandolier and shown how to load. He went over the ridge with the first wave and was killed going down the slope. A brave man.

The leading companies opened out into extended order. All the attackers advanced steadily and in disciplined lines over a smooth, rising slope of some 800 yards. It was a perfect field of fire for the machine guns on Mauser Ridge. As explained above, there was no artillery support at the crucial moment, and any that came into play later – provided by just eight Canadian 18-pounder field guns and eight British 4.5-inch howitzers – was far from adequate. The 1st and 4th Canadian Infantry (1st Canadian Brigade) and 3rd

General Erich von Falkenhayn (1861–1922)

Born into a West Prussian military family, Falkenhayn entered the army in 1880 and progressed steadily through the ranks of the officer corps. He served as an instructor to the Chinese Army from 1896 to 1903, and saw service on the Allied staff during the Boxer Rebellion in 1900. He returned to service on the Great General Staff and, in 1913, was made Prussia's Minister of War. He was a keen advocate of war in 1914 and, after the failure on the Marne, replaced Helmuth von Moltke as Chief of the Great General Staff. He initiated the 'Race to the Sea' that ended at First Ypres.

In 1915 Falkenhayn rejected the ambitious plans of Hindenburg and Ludendorff for a decisive blow on the Eastern Front, favouring instead a major attack on a sector not controlled by them. It was for this action that he allowed the gas weapon to be used at Second Ypres as a diversionary measure. In 1916 he began the deliberate policy of attritional fighting that led to the bloodbath of Verdun, and to heavy losses during incessant counter-attacks on the Somme. Having reassured the Kaiser that there was no chance of Romania joining the Allies, he was dismissed when they did!

He served brilliantly as GOC Ninth Army in the defeat of Romania, but suffered heavy defeat commanding Turkish forces in Palestine. He ended the war commanding Tenth Army in Lithuania. He wrote about his experiences and the problems of High Command after the war. He died in 1922.

Ever the strict military professional, with a contempt for parliament and democracy, Falkenhayn was withdrawn and unpopular. He could be both ruthless and indecisive, and his failure to reconcile the demands of the hugely popular duo of Hindenburg and Ludendorff for a complete victory over Russia, his own idea that Germany only needed to avoid losing the war in the west in order to 'win' it, and the collapsing German home front led to his downfall.

Middlesex were drawn into the attack to no avail. As A and C Companies, 3rd Middlesex, advanced in two waves 'by rushes' over 'absolutely open ground' they were caught by five machine guns hitting them in enfilade, with another two or three firing from their front. Within three minutes the whole of the first wave fell killed or wounded. Colonel Stephenson was mortally wounded and the two companies ceased to exist. Barely forty men survived the ordeal. Everywhere the British and Canadian infantry was cut down in swathes. Officer casualties were particularly heavy. B Company 2nd DCLI reached Turco Farm 'in time to find a German observer telephoning information of the attack. This gallant man stuck to his instrument and was killed with the receiver still in his hand'. It was all over by 7 pm, with the attackers gone to ground and trying to dig in where they could some 300 yards short of their target. Captain Bland, of C Company, 2nd KOSB, led one small party to within 200 yards of the German line but all were wiped out. Bland was killed as he tried to drag a wounded soldier back to safety. Of this battalion's officers only four junior subalterns emerged unscathed. Nine officers and 240 men fell in the attack. After dark, at about 9 pm, the survivors of the attack dug a line behind their forward posts and fell back to it without further loss.

That night a French battalion suddenly appeared and got into the already crowded trenches of 2nd DCLI. After a good deal of argument they were persuaded to get out and dig their own trench behind, which they did so closely that their parapet formed a parados to the British trench. 'Shortly after their arrival their cooks produced hot coffee which they shared with us. We were badly in want of it.' At about 10 pm 4th Rifle Brigade (on loan from 80th Brigade, 27th Division to Geddes Force), posted at Mouse Trap Farm and terribly impressed with the Canadians being so 'full of beans', was ordered towards the canal. By 11.30 this battalion had relieved the whole of the shattered 13th Brigade.

All the attacking battalions had suffered great losses – three colonels were killed; between eleven and eighteen officers, and from 200 to 450 other ranks per battalion were casualties. The 2nd DCLI lost three officers and forty-six men killed, seven officers and 216 men wounded, and six men missing in action. The 100 yards gained by the new trench line could have been gained at night with a fraction of the loss. The 2nd East Yorkshires told a similar tale, of a steady attack on a frontage of about 500 yards with two companies leading and two in support, each company deploying two platoons up and two following. Their attack strength of 640 rifles diminished rapidly under heavy enemy fire. With the limit of the advance still 100 yards short of the enemy, the order to retire was given. Only seven officers and some 280 other ranks made it back to the start line. Five officers and forty-two men were killed; nine officers and 256 men wounded; seventy-two men were reported missing in action. One small party, under Corporal Hall, did not hear the order to retire and pressed on to within 30 yards of the enemy front line. There they went to ground, scraping what cover they could, and lay for forty-eight hours within listening distance of the enemy, without food or water, before they all crept back safely to their own lines. As the historian, Brigadier General Ballard, explained:

> It had been hoped that Geddes would hit the flank of a confused line of infantry badly supported by guns. But the confusion was on our side. Geddes found himself crossing a mile of open ground, leading up to a well-organised defence. He had been committed to an impossible task. Undoubtedly the Germans had scored heavily in the matter of tactics.
>
> This first attempt had been something in the nature of an experiment, and consequently the higher authorities cannot be blamed for its lack of success. But it ought to have been sufficient to open their eyes to the true situation; there was evidence to show that the enemy could not be surprised; something more than mere weight of infantry would now be required to break that line. The French had no troops immediately available, and as the British had suddenly been forced to fill up a gap of 5 miles from the apex to the canal, all the local reserves had been used up. No further effort could be made without calling up fresh troops from other sectors, and this would weaken Joffre's strength for his offensive. It was no longer a case of redeeming a local and tactical situation; the solution demanded a wider outlook and a definite decision by supreme authority.

The sensible decision, short of the politically impossible one of abandoning Ypres altogether, was to fall back to a shorter, stronger defensive line immediately. This would free up troops from the elongated front of the Salient, move the artillery and rear area services westwards to safety, and allow the build-up of reserves to render the whole sector secure. Foch's obsession with removing 'the stain' of the lost French trenches would see more and more attacks over the same disadvantageous ground, which would use up British reinforcements as fast as they arrived in the Salient. Indeed, it would seem that the Germans had learnt the real lesson of the First Battle of Ypres (October–November 1914): that infantry could not 'crash through' a stubborn defence by sheer weight of numbers. Now they would not allow their infantry to outrun the support of their guns. They revived the tactics practised by their fortress troops, of limited objective attacks well endowed with artillery support. The gas weapon was developed as an auxiliary to this support. As in siege warfare, when the opposing trenches were so close together, or when the enemy front line could not be clearly defined, then the artillery switched its attention to the rear areas in an effort to choke off the flow of reinforcements, ammunition and supply to the line being attacked.

The Geddes attack had been made to redeem a promise to the French. To be fair to the French, they had endured a hard day's fighting as the Germans put the canal line under great pressure. Two German divisions had hammered at the canal line all day – 45th Reserve Infantry at Lizerne, and 46th Reserve Infantry at Boesinghe. A scheduled release of gas was poorly organised and the Belgian troops said it had little or no effect. The attackers were frustrated by the Belgian defence. Lizerne, near Steenstraat, was taken briefly but a counter-attack by the Grenadiers and Carabiniers of 6th Division retook the place. One battalion of Grenadiers held the hamlet while the other was in close support around the mill. The Germans finally seized the shattered ruins of Lizerne at about midnight. The Belgian Grenadiers alone lost ten officers and 453 men in the two days of fighting. French reinforcements, two infantry battalions and two batteries brought down from Nieuport, were immediately rushed to this sector to prevent further enemy advances. XXIII Reserve Corps War Diary was critical of the German troops:

Unfortunately the infantry had become enfeebled by trench warfare and had lost its daring and indifference to heavy losses and the disintegrating influence of increased enemy fire effect. The leaders and the brave-hearted fell, and the bulk of the men, mostly inexperienced reinforcements, became helpless and only too inclined to leave the work to the artillery and the trench-mortars.

The Belgian 1st Division had fed reinforcements in to help their 6th Division and their line grew stronger by the hour. German commentators regret that their High Command did not make this the main effort of the day, where they could have split the Franco-Belgian line and driven into the Allied rear. But the defence was stubborn and inflicted great loss on the attackers.

The BEF had committed every spare man available in the costly counter-attacks that put the Germans on the back foot for the day. But losses had been so severe that it greatly imperilled the chance of holding the line with any certainty. The Germans still had large numbers of unused gas cylinders in place. They spent a large part of 23 April planning how next to use them.

One eyewitness described just how critical the situation had been in the opening hours of the gas attack. Major John McCrae, the Canadian medical officer working at the Advance Dressing Station at Essex Farm, just west of the canal near Boesinghe, is now famous as the author of the iconic poem, *In Flanders Fields*. He wrote of the 'asphyxiated French soldiers' and crowds of civilian refugees, 'the very picture of a debacle . . . For 36 hours we had not an infantryman between us and the Germans and this gap was 1,200 to 1,500 yards wide. God knows why the Germans did not put in a big force to eat us up. We really expected to die'.

In Britain plans were being laid immediately for protective measures to be got out to the troops as soon as possible, and larger ideas about exacting revenge in kind were formulated. Maurice Hankey wrote to the Prime Minister: 'the normally prevailing wind in France is westerly, so that if this form of warfare is to be introduced we, in the long run, shall have an enormous advantage'.

*

Towards the end of 23 April the RFC had reported increased activity on the railways leading up to Menin and Ledeghem, and

Second Army alerted its formations to the danger of a renewed attack. Smith-Dorrien was warned by Sir William Robertson not to expect too much help from the French just yet, and Sir John French was still opining that 'vigorous action' east of the canal was still the best means of defence.

24 April: The Second Great Gas Attack

From 3 am 24 April onwards the Germans repeatedly attacked the Belgians along the canal, preceded by the copious use of gas shells. Not only did the Belgians defeat all attacks, but extended their line to the right to link more firmly with the French. The German infantry had reached a high-water mark on this part of the battlefield quite early in the proceedings.

At the very apex of the Salient, held by the Canadians, a heavy bombardment developed between 3 and 4 am. At 4 am, while it was still quite dark, another great gas cloud (15 tons of chlorine) was released on a 1,000-yard front. It quickly built into a fog bank 15 feet high and rolled rapidly over No Man's Land (from 100 to 300 yards wide). It struck the line held by Colonel Lipsett's 8th Canadian Infantry, and Colonel Currie's 15th Battalion. The attack was delivered by 4th Reserve Ersatz Infantry Regiment, backed by the rest of its brigade, and a composite brigade from 53rd Reserve Infantry Division (XXVII Reserve Corps). With two other brigades menacing the north-west face of the Salient, a total of sixteen German battalions were engaging eight Canadian battalions between Gravenstafel and Kitchener Wood, with only four companies in close support.

With just wet towels to protect themselves from the serious gas attack, many Canadian soldiers collapsed in their trenches. Remarkably, some two-thirds of the 8th (known as 'The Little Black Devils' in the Canadian Expeditionary Force) and three-quarters of 15th Battalion fought on very successfully. It seems that men who stood up on the parapet avoided the worst effects of the ground-hugging gas. The Germans made one small penetration of the line, where 15th Canadians (Royal Highlanders of Canada) were particularly badly hit by gas. When the 15th had lost all its front line officers, that battalion fell back in an orderly manner to its support line. German bombers tried to bomb along the trench against 8th Battalion to no avail.

43

The Gas Attacks: Ypres 1915

At around 5 am 7th Canadian Infantry could see wounded and gassed men of 15th Battalion falling back. Turner had to send for urgent help to 10th and 16th Battalions, both down to about 200 men after their ordeal in Kitchener's Wood. They had been resting in the defensive box known as 'Locality C' near St Julien, and came up to bolster the line. 2nd Canadian Field Artillery Brigade, firing at the very effective range of 3,500 to 3,800 yards did great execution to the attackers and protected the line of 2nd and 3rd Canadian Brigades. The heavy artillery behind Frezenburg Ridge also lent its support. The Canadians noted that, amongst the leading German attackers, one man carried a flag that was being used by German artillery observers to demark the line reached by their infantry.

The German infantry assailing the apex lost its enthusiasm for the attack. They went to ground and left it to their Marine Brigade to develop the attack against the north-west face. There the 13th, 7th, 3rd and 2nd Canadian Infantry and 2nd Buffs, free from gas and backed by heavy artillery, were presented with splendid targets, as the German marine infantry came in over level, open ground in close formation. They were beaten off with heavy losses. Ammunition supplies ran very low and the defenders had to reduce their rate of fire.

From 7 am the German attacks, delivered by a reinforced 51st Reserve Infantry Division, increased in intensity. Sustained pressure all along the line from the apex to Kitchener's Wood began to tell. By the penetration of 15th Battalion's line, 13th Battalion was threatened in the rear. They were forced to fall back at about 9 am, heading for 'Locality C'. In this difficult retreat, they lost almost 50 per cent of the battalion. B Company of the Buffs and two platoons of 15th Battalion couldn't get away and, after firing off all their ammunition, were surrounded and obliged to surrender. Suddenly a gap of 1,500 yards had opened in the front. Batteries of British heavy artillery stationed near the Menin Gate at Ypres were keeping the Germans on the Poelcappelle–St Julien road under heavy shrapnel fire. As the front crumbled they first moved their horse transport to the other side of Ypres for safekeeping, and the guns were obliged to follow.

Again the defenders reacted quickly to the emergency. By 7.40 am 150th Brigade (50th Division) had sent 4th East Yorkshires and 4th Green Howards up to assist, moving into the GHQ Line;

the rest of the brigade would follow before long. It was 11.33 am before Plumer realised the full danger and he allocated 10th Brigade (4th Division) and 149th Brigade (50th Division) to provide the basis for a counter-attack to restore the line later that day. 10th Brigade didn't arrive in Ypres until 8 pm after a long, hard march up from the south. They dumped packs and were on their way to the front line by midnight.

There was a brief pause in the attack, as the German infantry recovered its formation after the confusion inevitable in a series of converging attacks, during which they had lost heavily. After a heavy artillery preparation at 11 am, the attack was renewed along the line 'Locality C'–St Julien–Kitchener's Wood. The Germans came on in much more open formations with excellent support from their artillery and the aircraft spotting for them. The commanders of 7th, 14th and 15th Canadian Infantry met at a crossroads to decide their next course of action. They agreed to fall back to the western edge of the Gravenstafel Ridge, but were pressed very closely the whole time. 234th Reserve Infantry Regiment brought two field guns right up into their front line, firing at 200 yards range to blast a way through. The German reports speak respectfully of a determined resistance, and another Victoria Cross was awarded, to Lieutenant Edward Bellew, the Machine-gun Officer of 7th Battalion, for his defence of Keerselare (where the Canadian national monument stands today). When his machine gun was destroyed he continued to fire loaded rifles passed to him in relays. He was wounded and captured and, in the confusion of battle was accused by the Germans of fighting on after his unit had surrendered. For this he was brought before a firing squad, where he protested so vehemently that his sentence was commuted. Elsewhere that day CSM Fred Hall, 8th Battalion, was awarded a posthumous Victoria Cross for being killed in attempting to rescue a wounded comrade.

Disaster Looms

The British heavy artillery, reduced by shell shortages to an allocation of three rounds per gun per day, ignored the restrictions and did what they could with a collection of rather old and obsolete guns to support the infantry. The field guns of all three divisions of V Corps blazed away in defence of the line around St

Julien. Immediate reserves were desperately few and another disaster like that of 22 April loomed. Major General Snow (27th Division) was given executive control of the battle and sent his only reserve battalion, 1st Royal Irish Rifles, forward to secure Fortuin. The 365 men advanced a quarter of a mile in artillery formation up the slope towards Fortuin. They came under fire at 600 yards; the enemy had beaten them to it.

With renewed confidence, the Germans resumed their converging attacks on St Julien around noon. The Canadian defenders, though they were under orders to counter-attack and regain lost ground, knew it was all they could do to prevent the line collapsing. They were already forced back to the Gravenstafel–Wieltje Road, and only the stout resistance of 'Locality C' was keeping the Germans at bay. By 4 pm its garrison was down to one officer and thirty-seven men, and they were obliged to abandon the strongpoint.

Finally 3rd Canadian Brigade was ordered back into the GHQ Line covering Wieltje; 2nd Brigade was still defending its front very well. They were supported by sixteen guns of 2nd Canadian Field Artillery brigade. On 22 April these had 2,800 rounds at the gun positions and 1,200 rounds with the ammunition column in Wieltje. By the end of 24 April they had fired off 12,000 rounds, partly borrowed from neighbouring British divisions but mostly driven up from Ypres under conditions of extreme peril by the ammunition limber teams. The Germans eventually entered St Julien from the north at 3 pm, and from the west at 5 pm. They were pinned there for a while by the Allied artillery concentrating all its fire on that one point.

Meanwhile 152nd French Infantry Division had arrived along the canal, and its 306th Infantry Regiment attacked the German enclave at Lizerne at 8.30 am, and again at 2 pm. Though they failed to recapture it, they hemmed the German defenders in very tightly from three sides. It was a relief to see the long-promised French counter-attacks begin to manifest themselves.

Troops of 4th Rifle Brigade were impressed with the French Zouaves and Turcos that swept through their lines at about 2 pm. Then, in the first recorded instance of gas being used in a defensive capacity, they watched as a gas cloud formed over the German lines and 'rolled down the hill towards us like smoke'. The unprotected French infantry turned and bolted. 4th RB stood to and poured rifle fire into the cloud. Fortunately it was dispersing quickly in a diagonal wind, and the battalion reported some discomfort but no actual losses to gas poisoning. There was no German follow-up to the gas release.

Major General Snow (27th Division) took the bold step of commandeering, without asking, the reserves belonging to 28th Division (1st Suffolks and 12th Londons). He directed them, with two companies of his own reserve, 8th Middlesex, towards Fortuin, and 2nd Gloucesters were ordered up from Sanctuary Wood to reinforce the local reserve. Troops were being despatched to the critical point from all sides, but often they were units that were already sadly depleted in the fighting. Thus 2nd KOYLI and 9th Londons from 13th Brigade were ordered to join Geddes, and the two companies of 3rd Middlesex guarding the canal bridges were sent to rejoin their battalion with him. With a draft of sixty men, the survivors of A and C Companies, 3rd Middlesex, formed a composite third company and rejoined their battalion. When 2nd KOYLI went up to the line, north-east of Wieltje, to support the Canadians they found the trenches being so heavily shelled that they elected to lie out in the open fields behind the front. Inevitably they took heavy casualties, and only 250 men were under arms the next day.

But as they drew near to the scene of fighting these units were distracted from their counter-attack role and used to stiffen the line where most needed. Their approach march was always under artillery fire, and the nearer they got, the heavier the losses. The Suffolks had already suffered 280 casualties by the time they deployed; the Rangers (12th Londons) lost Colonel Bayliffe wounded, and sixty men. The Suffolks, who were on their way to Fortuin, received an urgent appeal from 2nd Canadian Brigade. On his own initiative their colonel responded, and sent two companies up to Boetleer's Farm, though the little force numbered just 150 men under a lieutenant. They found 7th and 10th Canadian Infantry there, down to 200 men between them. The Suffolks found themselves in the company of part of an ad hoc formation, typical of this confused and desperate phase of the battle. At around 5 pm six platoons of 2nd Northumberland Fusiliers had been pulled out of 28th Division's reserve and added to two companies of 2nd Cheshires and one of Monmouths, all under Major Moulton-Barrett of the Northumberland Fusiliers.

They were supporting 2nd Canadian Brigade by holding a crossroads midway between Zonnebeke and St Julien. Forming a line just north of the Hannebeke stream, Moulton-Barrett sent two platoons up to the front line. They arrived just in time to help the gas-stricken 8th Canadians beat off two German infantry attacks.

8th Battalion had appealed to 3rd Royal Fusiliers for help, but the latter were too weak to assist. Around 8.30 pm the Fusiliers passed the message to Moulton-Barrett. He sent all his Northumberland Fusiliers and it was these men who joined the Suffolks and did so much to close the gap between 2nd and 3rd Canadian Brigades and stabilise the line. At one stage a 3-mile gap in the British line was covered by the two infantry groupings around Moulton-Barrett and the Suffolks.

A Remarkable Performance by New Troops

At last two full-strength battalions arrived – 4th East Yorkshires and 4th Green Howards (50th Division). They went straight into the attack at 3 pm, Green Howards leading, and went forward 'as if they were doing an attack practice in peace . . . They went on in such a way as if they'd done it all their lives, nothing stopped them'. They bundled the Germans away from the Fortuin crossroads. They then went on and assailed the Germans who were debouching from St Julien. As the Green Howards reported 'we could find no one in superior command. We heard fighting going on towards St Julien and saw a few men retiring. We therefore changed front left and joined in.' Supported by the few guns to hand, they chased the enemy back into St Julien and were only stopped along the muddy banks of the Steenbeek. Joined later by the tough Regulars of Royal Irish Fusiliers, these young Northern Territorials earned the proud nickname of 'Yorkshire Gurkhas'. They had fifteen killed and sixty wounded in this, their first fight. 1/4th East Yorkshires had formed up in support, sheltering in a small wood. The private diary of Captain Sharp sets the scene:

We thought we were in for it, the noise was terrific and our artillery was shelled from each position they took up before they could get going. How the wood escaped I don't know, it was a trying time for our chaps. The Germans kept shelling a hamlet on a road to our front with, I should think, their 8-

inch Howitzers, an appalling thing, and very soon nothing
was left of it. The fumes from the shells blew over us and got
into one's eyes and were very unpleasant. It was now about
5 o'clock and still no news and nothing to do.

Then the battalion was ordered forward, moving through heavy
shellfire by platoons in extended formation of small section
columns ('artillery formation'), suffering ninety-eight casualties.
Captain Sharp again:

> Then came heavy Howitzer shells right amongst us which
> burst and made neat round holes about thirty feet by ten feet
> and threw up tons of muck when they hit a field. We were in
> small columns and sections and more than once sections
> were blown over by these hellish things. They were
> systematically spread over our advance and the men never
> faltered but went on and on – a splendid sight – they did
> magnificently, hungry and tired and weary tho' they were.

These young TF soldiers fired their rifles as they advanced, but it
had no marked effect on the German machine-gun fire sweeping
their ranks. Suddenly Lieutenant Colonel Shaw was shot through
the head – killed by a sniper. 51st Reserve Infantry Division wrote
up that it lost St Julien to a British counter-attack at 5.50 pm, and
they fell back to the heights north of the village. The threat of a
German breakthrough in the centre of the line was removed. The
arriving reinforcements were able to dig in and strengthen the line.
The British Official History remarks that this decisive intervention
did as much to save the day at Second Ypres as the Worcesters'
renowned attack at Gheluvelt on 31 October 1914. It counts it a
great disappointment that the action is not more famous. The
Division memorial stands near St Julien as mute testimony to this
extraordinary effort by such new troops.

The other two brigades of Northumbrian Territorials (149th
and 151st) were marching steadily towards Ypres, described as
'very fine troops' by those that saw them. Brigadier General Hull
was closing up with his 10th Brigade (4th Division) to relieve the
hard-pressed Geddes Force. Plumer wanted to pull his troops back
to a more defensible line in order to free up more reserves, but Sir
John French ordered him to make 'every effort' to 'restore the line

about St Julien'. Thus a naturally cautious commander was obliged to pursue a course that was anathema to him. Meanwhile Foch was badgering the British to give more support to the promised French counter-attacks. Yet when General Putz (always rather optimistic) was given the whole of the British Cavalry Corps, he selected just the Royal Horse Artillery units and dismissed the rest. How often had British attacks gone in with no sign of the French troops they were supposed to be assisting?

Order, Counter-Order, Disorder

The situation at the front was very confused, and there were a lot of frustrated troops receiving orders and counter-orders, in the rain and the dark, and often under enemy shellfire. 8th Durham Light Infantry (151st Brigade) were ordered to join 3rd Royal Fusiliers near Gravenstafel, to complete the digging of some trenches newly started there. They arrived, tired and more than a little hungry, with only their personal entrenching tools. The Fusiliers quite rightly said that they couldn't possibly start the job in the middle of the night, and they described the new trench as 'untenable'. 85th Brigade Headquarters promptly ordered the DLI into the front line to relieve 8th Canadians at Boetleer Farm. So, as dawn broke on 25 April, the DLI found themselves in trenches they were wholly unfamiliar with, and with the German front line at one point just 80 yards away, though No Man's Land averaged 250 yards. Being an old French trench, there were dead bodies incorporated in the walls and floor, and the sanitation was rudimentary. Instead of an orderly introduction to the finer points of trench warfare, 8th DLI were thrown in at the deep end. They even found themselves responsible for numbers of gassed and wounded Canadians who could not be moved. They endured heavy shelling all day, which fell most seriously on the two companies deployed behind the farm itself.

As the DLI took pressure off 8th Canadian Battalion, Moulton-Barrett brought his motley force back to their position just north of the crossroads. As the enemy bombardment continued relentlessly, troops that couldn't take the strain any more and had slipped away from the front line found themselves rallying on Moulton-Barrett's composite force. Together they worked to improve the position overnight, despite a steady rain that had set in.

Some very tired troops, not long out of an all too short rest from the fighting at Hill 60, were brought up to the St Jean–Wieltje area. One soldier of 9th Londons (QVR) described the experience, so very typical of men in war through the ages:

> We tramp across fields, recently ploughed and sown, passing the village of St Jean on our right. Everywhere troops are on the move . . . We stumble along as quickly as we can. I don't know who is leading us, or where we are making for. The air is thick with smoke and breathing becomes difficult . . . I reach a sort of 'don't care' mood and plod across to the trench as best I can, for I am absolutely whacked. I reach it in safety, and flop down on some straw in the bottom, thoroughly exhausted.

25 April

Plumer, under instruction from higher command, ordered Alderson to carry out a counter-attack that night, using 10th and 150th Brigades, and six battalions of his own troops. The trench reliefs of 3rd Canadian Brigade and Geddes Force were cancelled. All available guns were placed under the control of the Canadian Division's chief gunner. Orders were issued at 8 pm 24 April for an attack to be launched at 3.30 am on 25 April. It had been dark since 6.30 pm the day before, and it was raining heavily. Once again the executive control of the battle was passed down to a brigadier, C. P. A. Hull of 10th Brigade, who had to command fifteen battalions with only his normal brigade staff and no extra signals or army service troops. He was unfamiliar with most of the units under him, could not be certain of their whereabouts, or of the exact start line, and did not know the ground to be attacked. His instructions were to retake St Julien and Kitchener's Wood, to 'neutralise' the enemy artillery, and to push forward in a general northerly direction. Hull's own brigade marched up to Wieltje by 4 am, with no gas protection of any sort. There were so many delays for all the troops on all the roads that none were ready to attack before 5.30 am, when it was almost daylight. This report from 5th Durham Light Infantry, detailed with 5th Yorkshires (Green Howards) to support the attack, gives a sense of the difficult assembly:

> We set off along the Gravenstafel road, the 5th Yorkshires leading. It was a pitch-black night and pouring with rain; the road was crowded with limbers, G.S. wagons and ambulances going in both directions. The 10th Brigade were moving up the road at the same time as ourselves. We were evidently late, and our brigadier set a quick pace, with the result that the two battalions were stretched out over a great length of road. It was a difficult matter in the darkness and confusion to keep in touch. Here was a platoon well kept together, there two or three men acting as connecting files, further on a couple of men sent forward from a company further back, to try and get in touch with the company in front. One company commander kept his eye on the back of a private in front of him, and for some time flattered himself that he was 'in touch' only to find that the private was himself unattached! We passed through Wieltje, stinking with gas and the fumes of shells, and burning fiercely, the flames reflected in the pools of water on the road. At the road junction, the 10th Brigade went up to the left towards St Julien, while we went on towards Fortuin. Fortuin was found to be unoccupied by the enemy, and the two battalions halted and took up defensive positions on the north of the road . . . with a good field of fire towards St Julien.

In all the hurry and turmoil the 'shadow of defeat', to use another doom-laden phrase from the Official History, hung over the whole enterprise. Once again the delay in the start time of the attack was not conveyed to the artillery. The gunners duly fired their support barrage from 2.45 to 3.15 am, giving the enemy plenty of notice and time to prepare their defences. The gunners had been told that Canadians were holding out in St Julien still, and so they avoided it as a target. The machine-gunners of 51st Reserve Infantry Division watched as Hull's men emerged from a morning mist and advanced in perfect order towards them: 1st Royal Irish Fusiliers, 2nd Royal Dublin Fusiliers, 2nd Seaforth Highlanders and 1st Royal Warwicks led the attack, with 7th Argyll and Sutherland Highlanders in support, while 5th Gordon Highlanders went in on the right. Because they were so weak 2nd KOYLI, 9th Londons

(QVR) and 1st Royal Irish Regiment were kept in reserve. The Official History states that 5th DLI attacked on the right with the Gordons, but the battalion history makes it quite clear that they did no such thing. Their Brigadier had not been notified of the correct time for the attack and they watched the whole thing from their roadside trench. The attackers were 'deluged with fire', 'mown down like corn', and brought to a halt 100 yards short of St Julien. Some men of the Dublin and Royal Irish Fusiliers made it along a ditch to the outskirts of St Julien but were isolated there as their battalions were forced to ground. The RDF seized the last farm on the road up to St Julien and put it into a state of defence. One company had lost all its officers and was retiring as instructed but in some disorder:

> The small, untidy figure of Colonel Loveband, clad in an ancient 'British warm' and carrying a blackthorn stick, approached quietly across the open, making as he walked the lie-down signal with the stick. The effect was instantaneous, and for hundreds of yards along the front the men dropped and used their entrenching tools.

Loveband was wounded towards the close of the fighting, and handed command of the battalion to Captain Bankes. The Warwicks and Seaforths struggled to within 70 yards of a wood heavily defended by the Germans: here they were hung up and 'properly hammered' by German high-explosive shells, in the words of one who was there.

In a matter of minutes seventy-three officers and 2,346 other ranks – all of them irreplaceable trained men – were lost as casualties. At 9.45 am Hull reported to GHQ that the attack had broken down irrevocably. He implied that it would be the height of folly to order its renewal. Even Sir John French's bullish nature must have been tamed by this front-line opinion. The two Northumbrian battalions joined the move to the rear as 10th Brigade reeled back, but were ordered back to their trenches and held the line steady. Later they were ordered forward again to close up a gap, and suffered another 288 casualties for no apparent reason. The Germans were left free to improve their hastily dug line. They had posed no serious danger really. They were more interested in holding the ground gained than in pushing on. To their credit they did not interfere with the very busy British stretcher-bearers and medical officers as they went about their gruesome task on the broad slopes before the German lines.

In the Salient 25 April was a glorious day, with blue skies, warm sunshine, and a wonderful sunset. On that day, in Turkey, a hastily assembled and under-prepared Mediterranean Expeditionary Force carried out the first assault landing against modern, quick-firing weapons in military history. Their attempt to clear the Gallipoli peninsula would fail, and the addition of another battlefront to Britain's war effort would impose still further strains on her industry and resources. The men fighting in the Salient would suffer for it.

For the rest of 25 April the Germans tried to continue their attacks with little success. At 5 am they began a four-hour bombardment, mainly of shrapnel shell, of the lines held by 28th Division. Later the bombardment switched to gas and high-explosive shells. At 1 pm they assaulted the trenches held by 2nd East Surreys. The battalion reported that about fifty of the enemy got in at one point where 'the garrison had been rendered helpless by fumes'. A sharp counter-attack put them back out of the trench, leaving eight prisoners behind. Then A Company emerged from their dug-outs and flew at the retreating Germans, capturing an officer and twenty-eight men of 244th Reserve Infantry Regiment (XXVII Reserve Corps), and 'disposed of the remainder'. Joined by two companies of 8th Middlesex, they pursued the enemy into and along the German front line for about 150 yards before returning to their own trench. Of 240 Middlesex men, six officers and 100 other ranks fell in this impromptu counter-attack. The East Surreys also suffered for their success. Three officers and eighty-four men were killed in action; five officers and 119 men were wounded, with a further forty-three men posted as missing, believed killed. They were praised by their brigade and divisional commanders for the prompt manner of their sealing the breach and evicting the enemy. The enemy retained about 60 yards of captured trench, but 28th Division had defended its line well. The East Surreys, Royal Fusiliers and Middlesex beat off four separate infantry attacks.

To Retreat or not to Retreat?

That day 2nd Canadian Brigade got itself into a muddle. It, with two British battalions under command, had beaten off one attack in the afternoon, despite enduring very heavy shelling. The Canadians were running low on ammunition for their Ross rifles. The loss of their machine guns saw them lose some ground at about 6 pm. Hearing that reinforcements had been diverted to other work, Brigadier General Currie ordered the brigade to fall back: 8th Durham Light Infantry and 3rd Royal Fusiliers were not convinced that this was a legitimate order for them and refused to leave their trenches for the rear. Some Canadian infantry rejoined them in the front line. No one had any idea to whom 8th DLI were supposed to report. They had performed very well in defeating the various attacks delivered by the German infantry in a somewhat piecemeal fashion. On one occasion the Germans came forward wearing British khaki and calling out in English that they were 'British' and 'Suffolks'. When the Durhams came out of the line they had lost nineteen officers and 574 men in their first fight, and to think they went forward expecting to do a bit of trench digging. Pressure on the line built up to intolerable levels. Later that night the order to fall back was repeated and obeyed. By now 2nd Canadian Brigade was so reduced in numbers that it was officially relieved by just one battalion, 1st Hampshires (11th Brigade): 85th Brigade (28th Division) watched this withdrawal with some alarm, and had to form a defensive flank embracing Berlin Wood to maintain the line. As the Hampshires were digging overnight to improve their position, they were approached in the dark by men claiming to be 'Royal Fusiliers', a unit certainly known to be in the area. One credulous covering party was seized before another German ruse was detected and the intruders driven off by rifle fire. The wide knowledge and use of English amongst German troops had been utilised once again. A rush against the left-hand company of the battalion led to a fierce night battle before the line was stabilised.

The Official History finds no room for some of the small attacks made to slightly improve or stabilise the line. That evening 2nd King's Shropshire Light Infantry (80th Brigade, 27th Division) was 'loaned' to 85th Brigade. Two companies were sent up to the extreme point of the Salient, near Broodseinde, to retake a communication trench lost by the East Surreys. After a reconnaissance it was decided that just two platoons of Z Company, plus the machine-gun section, could do the job:

The enemy was too strong and the attack failed with the loss of all the officers engaged. Lieutenant Biddle-Cope, who was killed, was last seen standing on the German parapet, with a revolver in each hand, firing into the trench, having gallantly left his machine-guns, and rushed forward to join in the assault. Captain Bryant, who had a high standard of duty, and was absolutely without fear, also went over with his company, and reached the German line, where he was shot down. He succumbed later to his wounds in a German hospital, his widow afterwards receiving a letter from the German Staff praising his bravery. Lieutenant Blackett, another gallant officer, was killed, and Lieutenant Spink wounded.

Despite the admittance that 'artillery support was practically non-existent, owing to the shortage of telephone wire, and the impossibility of registering the batteries', and that 'efficient bombs and trench mortars were unfortunately not available at this period of the war', the regimental officers launched another charge at the same target. Lieutenant Evans led men of X Company over the very rough ground in another failed effort. He was wounded and taken prisoner. Thirty-two men were lost in these small attacks, having ascertained that the enemy had linked the communication trench to their own trench system and had moved several machine guns into position. Most Western Front battles were full of these desperate, and often hopeless, small-scale actions fought for some local advantage, and lost in the larger picture.

The Lahore Division Arrives

Elsewhere on 25 April the Germans made their last, unsuccessful, attacks on the canal line. They would not try their luck with the Belgians again. The British, seeing their fresh formations used up in a series of hopeless attacks, were still trying to build up a reserve: 11th Brigade (4th Division) arrived and was given to 28th Division. In a very difficult night march, in which more than one battalion stopped and dug in too soon, they were used to extend and solidify the line to the left, where the Canadians had fallen back. The 1st Rifle Brigade saw one of its companies deploy in the half-light and deliver a charge, only to sheepishly find they had 'stormed' an empty hedgerow! The Lahore Division (Indian Corps) arrived in the Salient after a 30-mile march over cobble-paved roads made slippery by the rain. They took casualties from shelling as soon as they reached the battle zone. Lieutenant Colonel Murray, of the Connaught Rangers, and his adjutant were severely wounded in the town, but 40th Pathans, who had only joined the division from China on 8 April, suffered the most. As troops marched through or past Ypres they all marvelled at the escalating level of destruction in the old town. 'The whole place seemed to be on fire', said one rifleman of 5th Londons (London Rifle Brigade).

Sir John French made sure that the Canadians understood that their fight had been appreciated. He insisted that only the German use of gas had forced them back at all. Their casualties had been very heavy – 1,700 killed; 1,800 wounded; 1,700 taken prisoner. Another Victoria Cross went to the Canadians as Captain Scrimger, Canadian Army Medical Corps, was rewarded for his selfless acts of devotion to the wounded, especially during the difficult withdrawals of the past few days (Captain Scrimger was one of the officers credited with the advice that urine might neutralise the effects of chlorine).

Sir John French had made it known to Foch that he thought the failures of French troops had got Second Army into difficulty, and he expected the French Army to get them out of it. Once again he pledged British support to a major French counter-attack scheduled for 26 April.

26 April

The continual pressure filtering down from Sir John French, via Smith-Dorrien (against his better judgement), on Plumer for decisive results saw the Lahore Division deployed straight from its column of march into the next attack. It was told to join a French attack at 2 pm on 26 April in a general northward move towards Langemarck. At least the attack was coordinated this time. Sir John French telephoned Smith-Dorrien in the late morning, to reassure him that he expected great things from this heavy joint attack. He – optimistic as ever – believed that the enemy was neither 'very strong or numerous, as he must have lost heavily and be exhausted'. Smith-Dorrien's private thoughts at these maddeningly 'upbeat' promptings must be left to the imagination.

British artillery supported the attack with fire from west of the canal. Because the exact location of the enemy trenches was not known (which did not bode well for the planned bombardment) some field artillery was placed at the disposal of the commanders of the two Indian brigades making the main attack. Two Canadian field batteries and a howitzer battery, and one field and one howitzer battery of the Lahore Division were available to provide direct fire support for the infantry as they closed with the enemy. This is a very early example of artillery being allocated to attacking infantry, something that is normally associated with the more sophisticated tactics of later war years. The Official History states that the artillery fired a forty-minute barrage, dictated not by the needs of the day but by the ammunition available. Infantry eyewitnesses doubt whether the bombardment lasted more than twelve minutes. Officially it ended with a five-minute 'crescendo', but this too was more theoretical than actual, and a barrage was placed 200 yards ahead of the attackers. There had been no pretence at wire-cutting and there could be no real support to the attacking infantry once they went 'over the bags'.

A Brigadier General Killed in Action

Elsewhere in the Salient all the British troops did what they could to engage the enemy to their front. In the GHQ Line 149th Brigade, under Alderson's temporary command, was detailed to take St Julien. The brigade, containing four TF battalions of Northumberland Fusiliers, had no opportunity to reconnoitre the area, and knew nothing of the other British troops in the area, and even less about the enemy to be attacked. They went in ten minutes ahead of the main attack, at 1.50 pm, and found themselves impeded by their own wire as they emerged from the GHQ Line. They complained that they were not carrying any extra ammunition and had only some thirty-five minutes to organise the attack, and found themselves flayed by enemy machine guns as they filtered through the uncut wire: 4th and 6th Northumberland Fusiliers led the advance; 7th Battalion was in support; 5th Battalion in reserve. They advanced in two lines, in the artillery formation they had practised so often in England, until the attack broke down at about 2.45 pm from machine-gun fire enfilading them from Kitchener's Wood. Great sacrifices were made in trying to cut the German barbed wire that impeded further progress. The 6th made the furthest advance, losing 119 killed and 499 wounded in the process; the 7th was drawn into the fighting line as the attack faltered. At 3.40 pm their commander, Brigadier General Riddell, was killed in action, shot through the head as he tried to get forward to speak with his battalion commanders. His brigade lost forty-two officers and 1,912 men – two-thirds of the attacking strength. A grievously wounded 149th Brigade dug in where it could. Its soldiers proudly boasted that they were the first Territorials to deliver a brigade-strength attack. As late as 1.25 pm, Brigadier General Hull had been ordered to join the attack. He looked at his battered 10th Brigade and, unlike so many other commanders, had the moral courage to refuse the suicidal order.

India to the Fore

The Lahore Division deployed the Jullundur Brigade on the right and the Ferozepore Brigade on the left, with the Sirhind Brigade in support. At 1.20 pm troops began moving forward to their jumping-off line. Packs had been dumped early in the day; greatcoats were now removed. The attack went in at 2.05 pm in full and plain view of the enemy. Some regimental officers were alarmed to find that their soldiers had been issued with new hand bombs with which they were wholly unfamiliar. Major Robertson, of 59th Scinde Rifles (Jullundur Brigade), exclaimed, 'So that was a pleasant situation, I must say, when we were just going into action!' The attack was so hurriedly prepared that information was both lacking in general and inaccurate in particular. The idea that the enemy trenches were not far away was soon disabused. After some 500 yards they breasted a slight rise and saw the enemy were anything from 1,200 to 1,500 yards off. The infantrymen were asked to carry little yellow flags to mark their progress for the artillery – they would provide excellent aiming markers for German machine guns. Advancing over exactly the same ground covered by Geddes Force in its unhappy attack on the Mauser Ridge, they found themselves mauled by enemy artillery from the very start and losses mounted steeply. Men fell in swathes as the German machine guns worked in perfect crossfire unison. From left to right the Ferozepore Brigade fielded the Connaught Rangers, 57th (Wilde's) Rifles and 129th Baluchis. The Jullundur

Brigade used 1st Manchesters, 40th Pathans and 47th Sikhs from right to left, with 59th Rifles and 4th Suffolks (TF) in support. Under terrific machine-gun fire the attackers were forced to their left, causing the men to bunch up, thus providing even better targets. As the troops trudged forward, the covering artillery barrage stopped, leaving them ever more vulnerable. The attack finally went to ground some 100 to 120 yards from the enemy line. 1/4th Londons (Royal Fusiliers) were following the Connaught Rangers when they witnessed a terrible sight. They commented on the paucity of their own artillery support:

> At 2 o'clock the attack was launched under a heavy bombardment from all available British and French batteries, but such was the shortage of ammunition that this support died down for lack of supplies in about five minutes, after which the German batteries were free to search intensively the whole area of the Brigade advance, causing a good many casualties in the assaulting columns.

Three German howitzer batteries near Langemarck reported firing 2,000 rounds that afternoon.

In about fifteen minutes the two attacking brigades had been shot to pieces. As a result, 40th Pathans had lost six officers and twenty-three men killed (including their colonel, mortally wounded), fifteen officers and 258 men wounded, with nineteen missing; 47th Sikhs lost seventeen out of twenty-one officers and 331 out of 423 men; 57th Rifles lost six officers and thirty-six men killed, eleven officers and 215 men wounded, with seven missing; the Connaught Rangers lost fifteen out of twenty officers (including their colonel wounded), and 361 out of some 900 men; 129th Baluchis lost an officer and eleven men killed, thirteen officers and 171 men wounded, with thirty-five missing.

At about 2.30 pm 4th Londons were getting into their stride, shaking out into four lines of platoons, two companies leading and two in the second line. As they breasted a rise overlooking the shallow valley towards Buffs Road,

> the sight which met their eyes defies description. The valley was covered with a ragged crowd of agonised and nerve-wracked men, both Moroccans and Indians, who, having

thrown down their arms and everything which could impede them, were streaming back from the front trenches suffering the tortures of poison gas. It was a revolting sight.

Some of the Connaught Rangers were caught by the gas and fell back in confusion. But as the Londoners passed through their ranks, Sergeant Udall heard one Irish NCO shout, 'Don't let the Territorials beat you!' Whereupon the proud Regulars turned about and went in again.

The French had delivered a heavy attack at 2 pm. At about 2.20 pm, as the British attack was faltering, the Germans had released a gas cloud against the right-hand French battalion. The French infantry pushed on through the dispersing cloud but were checked by fire and fell back to their supporting line. The gas also enveloped the wholly unprotected Indian troops in the Ferozepore Brigade. Most of the attackers fell back in disorder. To add to the tragedy, the machine-gunners of the Jullundur Brigade failed to recognise the uniforms of the fleeing French colonials (a light blue-grey, instead of the usual French dark-blue coat and red trousers), and poured fire into what they thought were pursuing Germans. Some sixty men of the Connaught Rangers under Major Deacon, fifty Manchesters under Lieutenant Henderson, and men of 40th Pathans, 129th Baluchis, 57th Rifles and 47th Sikhs held on in their scrappy new trenches. Corporal Issy Smith, 1st Manchesters, won the Victoria Cross here for rescuing wounded men under fire. However, 4th Londons, who had gamely trudged forward in perfect formation – as they had been carefully taught to do – could find no room in these trenches and had to dig their own line some 15 yards behind them. Later their commanders realised the trench was too crowded to be safe, and prepared another line some 300 yards back, to which about half the battalion retired. Orders were received at about 4.30 pm for the reserve company of the Connaught Rangers and two companies of 4th Londons to push forward and reinforce the new front line. The two brigade commanders took a realistic look at the open ground and the intensity of German shrapnel fire and could see nothing but pointless losses. The project was cancelled.

Heavy German counter-attacks forced the line back but one

remarkable Indian officer refused to give ground. Jemadar Mir Dast (55th Coke's Rifles, attached to 57th Rifles) gathered some men around him, even some gas victims, and held the front trenches for a little longer, allowing many men to escape to safety. When he finally retired at dusk his brave little band brought away eight wounded British and Indian officers. Mir Dast certainly earned his Victoria Cross, the fourth Indian recipient in the Great War to date.

Any movement in the fragmentary new front line brought down a storm of fire. The wounded were attended to under the most difficult circumstances. Because of the heavy casualties, especially in the Jullundur Brigade, two battalions of the Sirhind Brigade (1st Highland Light Infantry and 1/4th Gurkhas) were sent up to join them; 15th Sikhs were also needed, and finally, at nightfall, the whole of the Sirhind Brigade relieved the two attack brigades. They were pulled back to their start line, leaving many hundreds of fallen comrades behind them. Three battalion commanders had been killed and two more wounded. Both the Connaught Rangers and 40th Pathans lost all their officers killed or wounded. The new front line was consolidated by 3rd Sappers and Miners, and one company of 34th Sikh Pioneers. Those parties of Manchesters and Connaughts that had pushed on even closer to the enemy trenches were called back to a safer position.

When the French renewed their attack at 7 pm, three fresh battalions of the Sirhind Brigade joined them, but none of them progressed beyond the thin front line of the Lahore Division. The Lahore Division had lost 1,700 men without actually reaching the enemy front line anywhere. The 4th Londons were very impressed by the Turcos going in on their left:

A young French officer in charge of these Africans filled all who saw him with the deepest admiration of his coolness. Smoking a cigarette and lightly swinging a small rattan cane, he stood up on the sky line with his loose blue cloak thrown negligently over his shoulders, directing the advance of his men with all the indifference to danger of which his wonderful nation is capable. None of these gallant fellows were seen again.

Campaign Chronicle

The Germans Expected to Walk Into Ypres Today

Major Robertson, 59th Rifles, reflected on the battle and later wrote

> It seems that the Germans were expected to walk into Ypres that day, and indeed there was little enough to stop them. But whenever you sprung a surprise on Fritz he would pause while his staff did a bit of thinking. Here he was being attacked by Indians who ought to have been some 50 miles away, as they must have known. An obvious case for consideration! So they stayed where they were and lost their chance of walking in.

The French and Belgians had also attacked the German enclaves at Lizerne and Steenstraat without success. Very late in the day the French made one more attempt at Lizerne and stormed the German position there successfully. It would cost the French and Belgians almost 4,000 casualties to recover this desolate spot on the west bank of the canal. The German 204th Reserve Infantry Regiment was ordered to recover the position immediately, but they refused to leave their trenches. Their Corps commander said the French enemy were 'too numerous', but reports on his men said they 'lacked the right offensive spirit'. Quite simply the German infantry had had enough on that sector.

The Germans had made probing attacks against 85th and 11th Brigades without success. The defenders were, nevertheless, under unceasing pressure, 3rd Royal Fusiliers reporting that they were

> absolutely plastered with shell and every other kind of fire from three sides at once the whole time, with practically no assistance at all from our own guns, and nothing could exist or move over the ground in the rear, as every yard of it was plastered without ceasing by enormous shells.

The Fusiliers had already noted how effectively the German heavy artillery was impeding any supports or supplies getting up through Ypres by the incessant shelling of the town and the roads around it.

Meanwhile, on 28th Division's front, Moulton-Barrett's composite force awoke to find their 'support' position was now firmly in the front line. We have seen how 1st Hampshires had come up to relieve the Canadians and now the wretched 8th Durham Light Infantry were out in front as a sort of 'forlorn hope'. As they were remorselessly driven back by the Germans, Moulton-Barrett moved his command back some 400 yards to a more defensible line. He sent back to the Northumberland Fusiliers for two machine guns to secure his flanks. The Germans massed in front of the position and Moulton-Barrett was badly wounded and evacuated. The Adjutant, Captain Auld, was sent up to take command. He found just seventy Northumberland Fusiliers and Cheshires, plus two French 'poilus', lining a hedge. He sent a small detachment of Cheshires under a CSM forward to secure some farm buildings and 'scattered trees' to his front. The CSM was killed defending the position and men of the Northumberland Fusiliers went forward to assist. Auld sent an urgent appeal for reinforcements and received a very useful six machine guns and a company of 1st Welch. The Germans believed they were opposed by a very strong force indeed, such was the stout resistance they faced. The defenders would hold this line for two more days before being withdrawn, broken up and returned to their parent units.

The 1st Hampshires held their improved line all day under a relentless shelling that cost them fifty-nine killed and 100 wounded. Whenever the shelling slackened the men stood to arms expecting an attack but the local probing patrols were easily driven off.

In the general confusion of battle many small tragedies played themselves out. At 5 pm W Company, 2nd KSLI, was ordered forward about a mile to a ridge just behind where 28th Division's front line was under attack. They had to pass through gas and high-explosive shelling, and saw 6th and 7th Durham Light Infantry coming up in support. After a brief rest in some shallow trenches, the men of W Company were told to press on and relieve a section of the front in danger of being surrounded and overwhelmed. When they reached the spot 'no hostile infantry was met with, and the post, which was supposed to be in need of succour, was found holding its own quite unconcerned'. The 'relief' force was sent back, minus four men killed, and three officers and thirty-seven men wounded. The Germans resorted to shelling the British lines for sixteen hours a day, which was destined to continue for eight days without a break. Elsewhere the British and French could hear the sounds of Germans working busily in their trenches, which nowadays meant they were placing more gas cylinders for further attacks. German shelling made the resupply of forward troops and the evacuation of the wounded very difficult.

27 April: Smith-Dorrien Tries to Force a Decision From his Chief

When Smith-Dorrien was told of the French plans for 27 April, he remarked that they were only adding one new infantry regiment to the forces that had failed in their attack the previous day. He protested to Putz, and then wrote a long and detailed letter to 'Wully' Robertson, French's chief staff officer. This letter sums up the whole difficulty so well, and is such a well-argued case that it is worth giving in full:

My dear Robertson,
In order to put the situation before the C.-in-C. I propose to enter into a fair amount of detail.

You will remember that I told Montgomery (General Staff, GHQ) the night before last, after seeing General Putz's orders, that, as he was only putting in a small proportion of his troops (and those at different points) to the actual attack, I did not anticipate any great results. You know what happened – the French right, instead of gaining ground, lost it, and the left of the Lahore Division did the same, but the British regiment on the right of the Lahore Division, the Manchesters, did very well and took some enemy trenches and held them for a considerable time.

The Northumberland Brigade to their right made a very fine attack on St Julien and got into it, but were unable to remain there.

Away to the right between St Julien and our old trenches there was a good deal of fighting, but with fairly satisfactory results – the Germans usually retiring.

The enemy's losses are very heavy. Artillery observing officers claim to have mown them down over and over again during the day. At times the fighting appears to have been very heavy, and our casualties are by no means slight.

I enclose on a separate paper the description of the line the troops are on at this moment. I saw General Putz last night about today's operation, and he told me he intended to resume the offensive with very great vigour. I saw his orders, in which he claimed to have captured Het Sas, but on my asking him what he meant, he said the houses of that place which are to the west of the canal. He told me also that the success at Lizerne had been practically nil – in fact, the Germans were still in possession of the village, or were last night.

From General Putz's orders for today he is sending one Brigade to cross the river east of Brielen to carry forward the troops on the east of the canal in the direction of Pilckem, and he assured me that this Brigade is going to be pushed with great vigour.

It was not till afterwards that I noticed that, to form his own reserve, he is withdrawing two battalions from the east of the canal, and another two battalions from the front line in the same spot, to be used as a reserve on the bank of the river, so the net result of his orders is to send over six fresh battalions to the fighting line and to withdraw four which had been already employed.

I have lately received General Joppé's orders. He is the General commanding the attack towards Pilckem on the east of the canal, and I was horrified to see that he, instead of using the whole of this Brigade across the canal for the offensive, is leaving one regiment back at Brielen, and only putting the other regiment across the canal to attack – so the net result of these latter orders with regard to the strength of the troops on the east of the canal for the fresh offensive is the addition of one battalion.

I need hardly say that I at once represented the matter pretty strongly to General Putz, but I want the Chief to know this, as I do not think he must expect that the French are going to do anything very great – in fact, although I have ordered the Lahore Division to cooperate when the French attack at 1.15 pm, I am pretty sure that our line tonight will not be in advance of where it is at the present moment.

I fear the Lahore Division have had heavy casualties, and

so, they tell me, have the Northumbrians, and I am doubtful if it is worth losing any more men to regain this French ground unless the French do something really big.

Now, if you look at the map, you will see that the line the French and ourselves are now on allows the Germans to approach so close with their guns that the area east of Ypres will be very difficult to hold, chiefly because the roads approaching it from the west are swept by shell-fire and were all yesterday, and are being today.

If the French are not going to make a big push, the only line we can hold permanently and have a fair chance of keeping supplied, would be the GHQ Line passing just to the east of Wieltje and Potijze to join our present line about 1,000 yards north-east of Hill 60.

This, of course, means the surrendering of a great deal of trench line, but any intermediate line, short of that, will be extremely difficult to hold, owing to the loss of the ridge to the east of Zonnebeke, which any withdrawal must entail.

I think it right to put these views before the Chief, but at the same time to make it clear that although I am preparing for the worst, I do not think we have arrived at the time when it is necessary to adopt these measures. In any case, a withdrawal to that line in one fell swoop would be almost impossible, on account of the enormous amount of guns and paraphernalia which will have to be withdrawn first; and therefore, if withdrawal becomes necessary it must start gradually from the left. I intend tonight, if nothing special happens, to reorganise the new front and to withdraw superfluous troops west of Ypres.

I always have to contemplate the possibility of the Germans gaining ground west of Lizerne, and this, of course, would make the situation more impossible – in fact, it all comes down to this, that unless the French do something really vigorous the situation might become such as to make it impossible for us to hold any line east of Ypres.

It is very difficult to put a subject such as this in a letter without appearing pessimistic – I am not in the least – but as Army Commander I have, of course, to provide for every eventuality, and I think it right to let the Chief know what is running in my mind.

In this he was doing what the commanders of higher formations are supposed to do, thinking of the bigger picture and making timely suggestions. He was to receive a crushing response from GHQ, from a Commander-in-Chief who was clearly furious at the tone of the letter. The truth is that Sir John French would have accepted this wise advice from almost anyone in the world except Smith-Dorrien, whom he hated beyond all understanding.

In his diary entry for this day Sir John French had written: 'Smith-Dorrien, since the commencement of these operations, failed to get a real grip of the situation. He has been very unwise and tactless in his dealings with General Putz.' All major historians of this battle remark on the problems of working with the French. Cyril Falls simply says that the French 'did nothing' and the defence of the Salient was left entirely to the British; Liddell Hart described their support as 'negligible'. Sir John himself would later say that being allied to the French once in a lifetime was quite enough. While these all ignore a lot of hard fighting done by the French Army, they do refer to the many instances of the French asking for 'support' in making a counter-attack that they then find many good reasons for not making themselves. While Smith-Dorrien never personally defended himself from these slurs by his Chief, Brigadier General Ballard, in his biography of him, refutes French's charges line by line.

At 2 pm Robertson telephoned Smith-Dorrien with Sir John French's insistence that, with the abundance of troops to hand, the recent French success at Lizerne, and the preparations for a major Allied offensive in Artois, everything combined to make the situation less dangerous than it appeared. He demanded vigorous action in conjunction with the French. The phone call was followed up by letters delivered by staff officers to both Smith-Dorrien and Plumer. Smith-Dorrien's fraught relationship with his commander was reaching crisis point.

India Tries Again

The Lahore Division was ordered to support the next French effort, and the Sirhind and Ferozepore Brigades were given the task. Unfortunately the Sirhind Brigade, scheduled to wait for the Ferozepore Brigade to come up in line with them, jumped the gun and advanced as soon as the French artillery opened fire. The

Ferozepore Brigade hurried forward to catch them. Inevitably both suffered heavy losses from machine-gun and artillery fire and were forced to ground in the area of Canadian Farm. Major Burnett, 4th Londons, explained how he was called to brigade headquarters during the 'routine' German shelling in the morning and was given exactly thirty minutes' notice that his battalion was to take part in the attack. By the time he returned he had just ten minutes to point his battalion in the right direction and tell them to go:

> The hurried nature of the attack precluded any possibility of reconnaissance of the ground by the officers and allowed no time for explanation of the work on hand to the rank and file. The position of the German trenches was unknown and the difficulties and obstacles which might be met with during the advance were entirely undisclosed.

That the unit history referred to 'this unpromising enterprise' should come as no surprise. Their objective, Oblong Farm, was some 1,700 yards away and could not be seen. The attack of the Ferozepore Brigade was led by 4th Londons and 9th Bhopals, with the Connaught Rangers in support some 400 yards behind. The Sirhind Brigade led with 1/1st and 1/4th Gurkhas, with 4th King's (Liverpool), 15th Sikhs and elements of 1st Highland Light Infantry in support. From 12.30 they were under continual shelling and machine-gun fire. They had to cross broad, open country, with little shelter available. Every hedge and fold in the ground was known perfectly to the Germans and fire was expertly directed wherever troops might bunch up in the attack. Losses were 50 per cent in the leading companies of 4th Londons when they were forced to go to ground and dig in. The only surviving gun from their machine-gun section caught up and went into action near Hampshire Farm, helping greatly to suppress some of the enemy fire. The violent shelling increased and, under cover of darkness, the whole brigade was forced to fall back over about half the distance they had advanced. The Londoners had lost seven officers (four of them dead), thirty-two men killed, 132 wounded and thirteen missing. 1/4th Gurkhas had their CO, Major Brodhurst, killed and only three officers and some thirty men made it to a patch of dead ground about 200 yards from the uncut wire protecting the enemy trenches. The 4th King's made a determined advance by short rushes to join them, losing nine officers and a staggering 374 men in the process. Other battalions were being forced to go to ground between 250 and 400 yards from the enemy line. The 1/1st Gurkhas actually overran some French artillery pieces that had been lost to the Germans, and these were towed away safely that night.

The French had been so heavily shelled by the Germans that their infantry made no impression at all. But the enthusiasm of the French commanders for renewed attacks received a boost as their infantry completed the conquest of the German positions at Lizerne at about 4.30 pm, taking 250 prisoners. They then retook Het Sas and cleared the Germans from the west bank of the canal up to Steenstraat. The ferocity of this fighting should not be underestimated: 120 French officers and 3,853 other ranks fell in the battle to retake Lizerne.

The British were now so destitute of fresh formations that a 'composite brigade' of some 1,290 men drawn from 13th, 82nd and 83rd Brigades was placed under the command of Lieutenant Colonel Tuson (Duke of Cornwall's Light Infantry) and sent up into the line to support the Lahore Division. The four battalions had all been heavily engaged already – 2nd DCLI, 1st York and Lancasters, 5th King's Own and 2nd Duke of Wellington's.

Sir John French's Revenge

At 4.35 pm, in the midst of the battle, the axe fell on Smith-Dorrien. He was not dismissed as such but a plain uncoded message, clearly designed to heighten the degree of insult, was sent to his headquarters telling him to hand over the command of all troops fighting in the Ypres Salient to Plumer, leaving Smith-Dorrien to command only II Corps of his Second Army. His Chief of Staff, George Milne, was sent to Plumer, and was followed by his Chief of Royal Artillery and the rest of the army staff. Plumer was still GOC V Corps, and all the rest of the troops were designated 'Plumer Force' for the time being. The written instructions to Plumer asked him to consolidate his line and assist the French attacks, but also told him to prepare a line to the east of Ypres for a possible withdrawal, should it become necessary. This is, of course, the very thing Smith-Dorrien had suggested earlier that day, but this had merely exasperated Sir John French, who seized the opportunity to reduce Smith-Dorrien's influence. Their long feud had come to a head, and Smith-Dorrien must have expected the worst to follow.

In the midst of this organisational upheaval a fresh artillery bombardment was made at 5.30 pm and British and Indian troops made another hopeless charge to support the French: 1st HLI and 15th Sikhs dashed forward into a wall of fire of incredible violence. Lieutenant Colonel Vivian, 15th Sikhs, was killed; his second-in-command, Major Carden, was wounded soon after, only to be mortally wounded as he was carried away on a stretcher. The attackers could only go to ground and dig rudimentary shelter. The attack withered away under heavy fire before it even cleared the front line of the Sirhind Brigade. At 6.30 pm the Sirhind, Ferozepore and Tuson's Composite Brigades attacked again. They struggled through heavy fire up to the enemy wire. At 7 pm they saw the French colonial infantry on their left hit by poison gas (whether as a gas cloud or shells is uncertain). They broke and fled the field. General Putz actually appealed to the British cavalry to round up the fleeing troops, but they had already rallied around two steady battalions of Chasseurs. The British attackers tried to consolidate where they were but, with their left flank completely exposed, they were obliged to fall back to their start line. Regimental officers later thought how lucky they were that the Germans did not deliver an attack that evening. All the attacking formations were in a terrible state and would have been hard pressed to defend their positions.

The Lahore Division had lost another thirty-five British and eighteen Indian officers, and 1,152 other ranks, in another disappointing day. The British High Command consoled itself with thinking that their repeated attacks were pinning the enemy back and preventing any further penetration of the Salient.

Plumer started to get a grip on his disparate force. He ordered the unwieldy 'Geddes Force' to be broken up and the units returned to their parent formations. Colonel Geddes had been pitchforked into the most desperate situation, and had done all that was humanly possible to shore up a seriously weak line in some very hard fighting. In a tragic turn of events he was killed outright the very next day when a German shell crashed into the room where he was resting. Once 27th Division recovered its units it was able to free up two battalions as a corps reserve. Elements of 50th Division were moved to support 28th Division. German prisoners were speaking of how weary their units were, being asked to attack over and again without substantial reinforcement. When the French announced at 9.15 pm that they would renew their attacks on 28 April, Plumer consciously vowed to wait and see how they progressed before committing his own exhausted troops to any further efforts. After two gruelling days in the support trenches behind the Sirhind Brigade, Tuson's units were returned to their parent formations. Supposed to go into rest, 2nd DCLI soon found themselves digging in the fallback positions then being prepared; 1st Leinsters, who had 'a fine reputation in digging', found themselves similarly engaged for several nights in a row.

Still the fighting flickered along the front of 28th Division. That evening 2nd KSLI were ordered to try again and capture the communication trench that had defeated them on 25 April. More preparation was allowed this time. The two companies, 140 and ninety strong respectively, were given clear objectives, and were able to use old trenches to get within 100 yards of the enemy line. Artillery support was organised and, at 2.40 am on 28 April, the attack was delivered. It was a clear, moonlit night and the attackers hoped to cross the short distance quickly. The Germans held their fire until the attackers were within 30 yards and poured in a devastating volley: few reached the parapet. All the officers fell, one killed, two wounded and one captured; twenty-three men were killed and twenty-eight wounded. The battalion was returned to 80th Brigade. They remarked ruefully that an entire brigade would later fail to take the same trench.

28 April: A Slight Pause

The Germans were waiting for a favourable wind to deliver another gas attack, supported by the newly deployed XXII Reserve Corps. The Allies would take some prisoners from this new formation later in the day and so were made aware that it had come down from the north. The RFC spotted more German heavy guns being moved into position, and intelligence reports were received identifying some 8,000 German infantry drafts arriving at Ghent and moving forward from there. So, while the day passed without any major German attacks, the enemy artillery pounded away ceaselessly, and Plumer knew to expect more trouble before too long.

From dawn until about 3.30 pm the French artillery bombarded the Germans along the canal. The shelling was described as 'spasmodic' by the Belgian and British artillery lending their support. The subsequent attack on Steenstraat was really quite weak. On the left three French regiments attacking Steenstraat were shot to pieces while still 500 yards from the enemy line. In the centre and on the right French troops fired but did not advance at all. The weight of German fire negated the effort everywhere. The British on the east bank had learned their lesson and did not stir from their trenches until they saw how the French fared.

The Decision to Withdraw

Instead, at 10 am, Sir John French told Plumer to go ahead with serious plans to withdraw to a more defensible line, perhaps even that very evening. Plumer had selected a line running from Hill 60, via the Menin Road just in front of Hooge, then along Frezenburg Ridge to Mouse Trap Farm, and then back to the canal. He warned it would take four nights to complete the withdrawal, provided no more wasteful attacks were ordered, and then he did not guarantee that the new line could be held for long. When Foch heard of this plan he protested violently to Sir John French. The latter promised to delay the withdrawal of the front line, but declared the Salient, as it was, to be untenable, and gave orders for the evacuation of surplus units to go ahead forthwith. Liddell Hart is scathing about this ambivalent attitude: 'The days that followed were a comedy behind the front, a tragedy for the troops in the front.' Declaring that a reduced salient would be 'one huge artillery target', Liddell Hart went on:

> The political and sentimental objection to yielding ground, especially Belgian ground, and the military desire to facilitate the task of any belated French effort, led Sir John French to override the fighting commanders' wish to withdraw to the natural straight line of defence formed by the ramparts of Ypres and the Canal.

Even the British Official History insisted that small losses of ground should be accepted without wasting lives to retake it, especially when larger offensive efforts were being planned elsewhere. It gives the loss of Vimy Ridge in 1916, just before the Somme offensive as a case in point. The hasty counter-attacks 'invite failure and run the risk of heavy casualties without any compensating success'. It concludes that the Salient should have been evacuated earlier and more completely.

When the French announced that their planned attack for 29 April had been cancelled, it came as no surprise – and something of a relief – to the BEF. The French artillery, always well endowed with ammunition, was still weak in actual numbers of guns and was waiting for new batteries to come into the line and register. It was quite galling for Foch to issue demands for more 'simultaneous, not successive, efforts of British and French troops'. That is what the BEF had been hoping for since 22 April. His demand for more energy and coordination fell on sceptical ears.

Plumer continued to plan his staged withdrawal to the new line that was being dug each night. Each day of relative calm, incessant enemy shelling excepted, was a bonus. Having been released by First Army, 7th Division was arriving in the Salient as a welcome reinforcement. Meanwhile the battalions of 50th Division, supposedly getting a rest, found they were in great demand: hailing from some of the great coalfields of England, they were detailed for digging work on the new trench systems. Ironically, while the infantry were put to laborious duty, the Division's engineers and pioneers were kicking their heels well behind the lines. They were eventually employed digging various switch lines to bolster the defences around Ypres.

At 6 pm the French stormed Steenstraat village and now the Germans only held one single trench line west of the canal. The problem now was that the lines were so close together that artillery support was as big a danger to the attackers as to the defenders. Next day the French would make some small gains along the canal bank.

29 April

The day of 29 April passed without any major upheaval. Thick fog prevented the French attack going in at 8 am. When told that it would commence at 11.15 am, Plumer ordered British artillery to support the bombardment, and the Sirhind Brigade was alerted to be ready to assist if the attack developed well. On seeing that the enemy wire was not cut, the French attack did not develop at all. When General Putz asked if the Sirhind Brigade would join an attack on Hill 29 (Mauser Ridge), Plumer made it quite clear that they would do so only if the French absolutely guaranteed that the attack would go in properly. The lesson of uncoordinated attacks had finally been learned.

The British continued their preparation for the evacuation of the apex of the Salient, despite Foch's objections. Meanwhile 12th Brigade arrived to complete the concentration of 4th Division at Ypres. This at least gave the battered 13th Brigade – down to 1,400 fit men – a chance to get a rest out of the firing line to the west of the canal. The Jullundur and Ferozepore Brigades were also pulled out of the Salient and sent back for a rest.

30 April

An entry in Sir Douglas Haig's personal diary tells us just how bad things were between Sir John French and Sir Horace Smith-Dorrien:

> Sir John also told me Smith-Dorrien had caused him much trouble. 'He was quite unfit, he said, to hold command of an Army' so Sir John had withdrawn all troops from his control except the II Corps. Yet Smith-Dorrien stayed on! He would not resign! French is to ask Lord Kitchener to find [Smith-Dorrien] something to do at home . . . He also alluded to Smith-Dorrien's conduct on the retreat and said he ought to have tried him by Court Martial, because [on the day of Le Cateau] he had ordered him to retire at 8 am and he did not attempt to do so.

1–7 May: The Salient Shrinks

The Sirhind Brigade Goes in Alone

On 1 May Plumer did agree to support a French attack and, once again, the Sirhind Brigade was alerted for the task, and 28th and 4th Divisions were instructed to support the attack if it went well. But at 3.10 pm, after a preliminary bombardment, the French infantry did not leave its trenches. The same thing happened at 4.40 pm. A British liaison officer said the French infantry were 'too tired for any further serious effort'. Mercifully 'Papa' Joffre had intervened and ordered the French Army in the Salient to go over to the defensive. He did not want reserves drained away from the upcoming Artois offensive. Tragically, this was not known to the Sirhind Brigade who had, obediently, attacked under the cover of the guns at 2.50 pm. The two Gurkha battalions (1/1st and 1/4th) tried a new way to cope with the inevitable ordeal. They stripped away their equipment save weapons and ammunition and ran like the devil down the slope towards the enemy. As they passed the front line 15th Sikhs cheered this amazing display. By speed alone they outwitted the German artillery observers and got within 150 yards of the enemy before small arms and machine-gun fire drove them to ground. Casualties had been remarkably few when compared to other attacks over this same ground. Still, with the supporting units – 4th King's and 1st HLI – another nine officers and 250 men were lost to the brigade. *Kukris* were not able to cut the German wire. The Gurkhas held on till nightfall, engaged in bombing duels with the better-supplied enemy.

British GHQ formally ordered Plumer to begin the withdrawal from the apex, to commence at 8 pm. That night the Lahore Division was pulled back across the canal, having lost 24 per cent of their strength, 3,889 officers and men, in under a week. Half the Canadian artillery still in the area, and 123rd Battery RGA also went over to the west bank. Half 27th Division's artillery fell back to the canal. Everything was carried out without any undue loss. Units that had been through the heavy fighting found themselves absorbing large drafts of new replacements from the infantry depots in France and Great Britain; 2nd Buffs received 150 in one go just as they were about to go back up the line. They didn't have time to absorb them into the various rifle companies, so they grouped them all in one company and made sure it was posted in the relative safety of the support line. There was not even time to record all their names in the battalion's papers before they were sent up the line.

Campaign Chronicle

Gas at Hill 60

Over on the right fighting flared up at Hill 60 as the Germans took advantage of favourable winds for another gas attack. At some points the front line here was barely 40 yards from the enemy. While this reduced the amount of shelling on a daily basis, it made the area lethal from the persistent sniping and the close use of hand grenades and trench mortars. Once again an eerie silence from 4 pm spelled an impending outbreak of violence. From 6 pm to 7 pm the Germans shelled the hill heavily, hitting 1st Dorsets (15th Brigade, 5th Division) – who had only just relieved the Devons – very hard. Then, according to Company Sergeant Major Ernest Shephard, began 'the most barbarous act known in modern warfare'. On a quarter-mile front the Germans released a gas cloud from sixty cylinders that quickly covered the 100 yards of No Man's Land, catching the defenders as they fumbled to put their wet pads over their mouths and noses. In the absence of proper masks a wet handkerchief was recommended. Captain Ransome wrote dismissively: 'It is true to say that none of these expedients were of the slightest use.' One company was caught with dry pads and suffered particularly badly. Men instinctively crouched down in the trenches, which was the worst way to cope with the ground-hugging gas. It took great presence of mind in the chaos of battle to remember the encomium to breath in through the wet mask and exhale through the nose. CSM Shephard's diary account explains why the British soldiers were so outraged by this development in the war:

> the enemy . . . started pumping out gas on us. This gas we were under the impression was to stupefy only. We soon found out at a terrible price that these gases were deadly poison. First we saw a thick smoke curling over in waves from the enemy trenches on the left. The cry was sent up that this was gas fumes. The scene that followed was heart-breaking. Men were caught by fumes and in dreadful agony, coughing and vomiting, rolling on [the] ground in agony. Very shortly after gas was pumped over to us, the enemy were seen running from their own trenches as a part of the fumes blew back to them . . . Men caught by fumes badly were at this stage dying, and we fully realised our desperate

position . . . When we found our men were dying from the fumes we wanted to charge, but were not allowed to do so. What a start for May. Hell could find no worse the groans of scores of dying and badly hurt men, the chaos which, however, soon gave way to discipline, the fierce fighting and anxiety.

The next day he continued with this bitter entry:

several of my best chums are gone under. Had we lost as heavily while actually fighting we would not have cared as much, but our dear boys died like rats in a trap, instead of heroes as they all were. The Dorset Regiment's motto now is, 'No prisoners'. No quarter will be given when we again get to fighting . . . I feel quite knocked up, as we all are, and crying with rage.

In fact the Dorsets held their parapet, despite their heavy casualties. Captain Lilly, commanding A Company on the right by the railway cutting, recalled having to heave dead and dying men out over the parados of the trenches to make room for men firing from the firesteps. He remembered his brass buttons turning quite black from the effects of the gas and thought that the sheer amount of activity in clearing the trench for action might have helped disperse any lingering gas. One of his junior officers, Second Lieutenant Mansel-Pleydell, had just emerged from a dug-out when he

saw a hose sticking over the German parapet, which was just starting to spout out a thick yellow cloud with a tinge of green in it. The gas came out with a hiss that you could hear quite plainly. I at once shouted to my men to put on respirators (bits of flannel), then I got mine and went and warned my captain.

He also saw the wind catch some of the gas and blow it back onto the German trenches, causing some pandemonium there. Pushing upwards into the firing line was the best thing for the defenders to do. So many men fell back down the hill in the first throes of gas inhalation, only for the gas to flow down after them and finish their death agonies. The young subaltern spoke of the anguish he felt:

> I was simply mad with rage, seeing strong men drop to the ground and die in this way . . . I saw two men staggering over a field in our rear last night, and when I went to look for them this morning they were both dead . . . I am absolutely sickened. Clean killing is at least comprehensive, but this murder by slow agony absolutely knocks me. The whole civilian world ought to rise up and exterminate those swine across the hill.

But the most remarkable feat of heroism was displayed on the crest of the hill by Second Lieutenant Kestell-Cornish (a nineteen-year-old straight out from Sherborne School) and the only four privates with him not affected by the gas, who together climbed up onto the parapet (an excellent way of avoiding the worst of the gas) and blazed away with rifles into the gas cloud. The Germans assumed this vital part of the line was strongly held and did not press home the attack there. The Dorsets' CO, Major Cowie, instantly awarded Kestell-Cornish the MC, and his whole party were rushed off to the dressing stations to be treated for gas inhalation. (Kestell-Cornish would remain for just one week in hospital before insisting on returning to his battalion. He would win a bar to his MC, serve as a staff officer with 32nd Division and die of wounds in 1918.) When 1st Devons and 1st Bedfords charged up through the gas clouds, then about 3 feet high and dispersing, together they inflicted the first clear defeat on a gas cloud attack. A Victoria Cross was awarded to Private Edward Warner, 1st Bedfords, though he later died of gas inhalation. He had entered a trench to defend it against the enemy and found himself alone there. He pushed his way through lingering pockets of gas to guide more men onto the position, thus securing it for the attackers. Ninety Dorsets had died from gas in their trenches. Of the 207 gas casualties evacuated, a further forty-six died soon and another twelve more later. The thirty-two posted as missing were mostly found to have crawled away and died alone from the gas.

The Gas Attacks: Ypres 1915

A Major Gas Attack

It seems that only unfavourable winds prevented a general gas attack on the Salient on 1 May. The conditions were more suitable on 2 May. For most of the day the British were able to surreptitiously continue planning their withdrawal. Around noon a heavy enemy bombardment of the north face of the Salient was commenced, falling mainly on 4th Division and the French. From 4 pm to 4.30 pm gas shells were used, and at 4.30 pm a gas cloud was released on a 3-mile front. The Germans later made clear that the attack was related entirely to a favourable wind and was not influenced by British withdrawals, of which they seemed unaware. The attacks were determined only by the availability of gas cylinders and the right wind to use them.

The 51st Reserve Infantry Division attacked with its 102nd Reserve Brigade south of St Julien, its 101st Reserve Brigade at Fortuin and the attached 2nd Reserve Ersatz Brigade on the Langemarck–Zonnebeke Road near 'Locality C'. The 53rd Reserve Infantry Division sent its 105th Reserve Brigade in west of the Ypres–Langemarck railway, and one regiment of the attached 38th Landwehr Brigade in south-west of St Julien. The 52nd Reserve Infantry Division was supposed to join this main effort but found itself defending against a spirited French attack. The reports by the attackers complain of the squally wind and the uneven distribution of the gas cloud. They also remarked that the British seemed very alert and ready to receive the attack, and possessed of much improved anti-gas protection. Their claims that the British defences were formidably strong, with deep wire entanglements, smacks rather more of excuse than explanation.

The gas took just two or three minutes to cover the 150 yards of No Man's Land, and passed over the lines in about fifteen minutes. It hit the left of 10th Brigade, the whole front of 12th Brigade and the right of the French positions east of the canal: 10th Brigade stopped the attackers in their tracks; 12th Brigade was badly hit. The 2nd Lancashire Fusiliers alone suffered 449 gas casualties and part of their trench was lost. Fusilier John Lynn had rushed to man his machine gun so quickly he did not have time to put on his gas mask. He poured fire into the approaching cloud and, as the fumes began to overcome him, he hoisted the gun up onto the parapet to get a better field of fire. No Germans reached his part of the trench. A posthumous Victoria Cross was awarded to him.

The 7th Argyll and Sutherland Highlanders, one company of 5th South Lancashires, and 4th Hussars and 5th Lancers sent up from reserve positions near Potijze all rushed up through the dispersing gas to stiffen the line and assist the Lancashire Fusiliers in beating off the attack. The 1st King's Own not only beat off the attack but pushed a platoon forward into some houses to pour enfilade fire into the enemy. The 2nd Essex lost part of their line but their own supports came up and recovered the ground lost. Their heavy losses – eight officers and 265 other ranks – included three officers and 175 other ranks gassed.

The French also beat off their attackers. French and British artillery laid very effective barrages behind the gas clouds, and the RFC directed British heavy artillery fire onto approaching German reserves. For the first time a major gas attack had been halted in its tracks. The careful use of counter-attack units had evicted the enemy where Allied rifle and machine-gun fire had failed to keep them at bay. Brigade headquarters were well placed to keep a firm grip on the battle. Important lessons in effective defensive fighting were being learned and applied.

The battle died down by 8 pm, to the intense annoyance of the unsuccessful Germans. They would wait for another favourable wind before their next main attack. From 9.45 pm Plumer resumed his withdrawal programme: 2nd Cavalry Division, two brigades of 50th Division (149th and 151st), half 28th Division's artillery, five batteries of Canadian artillery and one of 27th Division's Field Artillery brigades were all got away in one moonlit night. The French were also able to pull one infantry division out of their line. Only the infantry component of 27th, 28th and 4th Divisions, supported by some field artillery, remained in the old front line, waiting their turn to retire to the prepared positions behind them. The men of 150th Brigade were still serving with various other formations in the front and support lines and, while not directly involved in any fighting, their losses crept up and up. The 4th Green Howards lost thirty-four killed and eighty-one wounded or gassed on 2 May; 4th East Yorkshires lost ten killed and thirteen wounded on 2 May, and a further twenty-three killed and forty-seven wounded on the 3rd.

Preparing to Withdraw

The Germans must have sensed something was afoot for the overnight shelling of the apex of the Salient in and around Berlin Wood intensified, falling mainly on 85th and 11th Brigades. The British artillery – just five field and three howitzer batteries – was singled out for heavy pounding. From 7 am on 3 May the British infantry could see German infantry pressing down towards them from Passchendaele, cutting lanes in their wire and lying out in No Man's Land, prior to an assault. German official records simply say 'the action was stopped on the 3rd, and the continuation of the offensive was only to be resumed after further preparations'. This bland report covers the complete destruction of the German infantry attacks of XXVII Reserve Corps by the deadly efficiency of the rifle and machine-gun work of the British Regular infantry. All the early attempts to charge the British lines were shot to pieces. The Hampshires, in common with many battalions, said what a relief it was when the German infantry finally attacked. After helplessly enduring intense artillery bombardment, it was good to be able to use one's personal weapons to such good effect. In particular, 39th Field Battery RFA (XIX FA Brigade) did 'great slaughter' with shrapnel shells amongst the German infantry that it caught in the open. Royal Engineers working close by acted as ammunition carriers for the guns, to help them keep up their rate of fire.

At 2.55 pm a ferocious bombardment fell upon Berlin Wood, where the men on the receiving end said the shells rained down like machine-gun fire. The young drafts so recently absorbed by 2nd Buffs held up well under the ordeal. Then two heavy infantry assaults struck the lines of 2nd Buffs and 1st Rifle Brigade (4th Division). In the first stage of the fighting the Germans captured Berlin Wood but the British kept their line intact fighting from the support trenches. German infantry rushed one trench held by the Buffs. Its garrison of a captain, a lieutenant and eighty men of C Company simply vanished without trace. The Germans were able to enfilade other British trenches from this vantage point, and both the Buffs and 3rd Royal Fusiliers were forced to give ground. Two men of the Buffs acted as a rearguard, keeping the enemy at bay during the withdrawal, before making their own escape. Major Power was badly wounded in the chest leading forward the reserve

Erich von Falkenhayn, Chief of the German Great General Staff, who instigated the use of poison gas, merely as a diversion to permit the transfer of German troops to the Eastern Front.

Duke Albrecht of Württemberg, commander of German Fourth Army, was a typical product of the German military system. Guided by a competent Prussian chief of staff, his army carried out the attacks from 22nd April to 24th May 1915.

Marshal Joffre, Commander-in-Chief of the French armies on the Western Front. He could afford little help to the Ypres Salient as he was preparing the great spring offensives in Champagne and Artois.

Lieutenant General Sir Herbert Plumer, commander of V Corps and then Second Army. Never judge a book by its cover! While looking like a 'Colonel Blimp', Plumer was the most careful and competent of all Britain's Western Front generals.

Sir John French, Commander-in-Chief of the British Expeditionary Force. Though senior to Foch, he was completely in thrall to him, and forced his generals into pointless and bloody attacks to recover lost ground.

Crown Prince Ruprecht of Bavaria, commander of German Sixth Army. His warnings that Germany would be at a grave disadvantage once the Western Allies developed gas weapons of their own were ignored. He was right.

Ferdinand Foch, commanding the French troops in the north. This pugnacious and aggressive soldier was principally responsible for the costly and futile counter-attacks in April and May 1915.

General Sir Horace Smith-Dorrien, commander of British Second Army. This brave fighting general was detested by Sir John French, who took the earliest opportunity to have him replaced.

The Germans published this picture, supposedly of victims of an Allied gas attack, to justify their use of poison gas. In the 1920s they would apologise for the blatant untruth that the Allies used it first.

Belgian machine-gunners in the earliest mouth-and nose gas protectors

A French soldier of 1915 manning a trench, wearing one of the early gas masks.

French victims of the gas attack at Langemarck on 22nd April 1915. While we talk of 'trenches', this picture shows that field defences were more barricade than excavation in the wet Flanders fields.

These 'Tommies' at work are wearing a very crude early form of gas protection.

On gas sentry duty at St Julien, this British soldier is keeping his gas mask handy for quick use. Let us hope the pet dog is not there in the role of the miner's canary!

—Sketch showing Bottle and Rubber Pipe—
—used with Asphyxiating Gas.—

The Royal Engineers of Second Army soon identified the German method of delivering poison gas in cloud attacks, and distributed this sketch of the equipment to Allied formations.

A gas cloud attack on the Western Front. This is actually a French photograph from later in the war, but gives the only impression we can have of the first attacks in April and May 1915.

This photograph of German 'stinkpioniere' shows them preparing a gas attack, concealing and weighting the pipes down with sandbags on the parapet.

'Second Battle of Ypres 1915' by Richard Jack, Canada's official war artist. This is a typical piece of official, heroic war art, with some small inaccuracies, but conveying the splendid achievement of the Canadian troops who faced a gas attack on 22nd April with no protection whatsoever.

Another famous portrayal of Canadian resistance to the first gas attack, giving a good indication of the power of German artillery to smash down field defences.

A powerful work by Fortunino Matania showing the real horror of poison gas. This picture appeared on the front cover of *Sphere* magazine, 29th May 1915, entitled 'How the Gas Devil Comes'.

'Afternoon Tea in the Salient' shows how exhausted officers could get little in the way of real rest during Second Ypres.

British victims of gas attack. Though almost certainly from later in the war, it shows how the effects of gas were often more incapacitating than fatal.

The iconic Cloth Hall, Ypres, in the early stages of its complete destruction by German artillery.

St Julien under German occupation in 1915. It was the focal point of resistance in April, and would not be retaken until 1917.

A man-portable *Kleinflammenwerfer* as used at Hooge on 30th July 1915.

company of the Buffs, but the line was stabilised and held. The history of the Rifle Brigade recounts how 1st Battalion had to watch helplessly as a German field battery deployed in the open about 1,000 yards off and opened a most destructive fire on their trenches. The British artillery simply didn't have the ammunition to deal with that particular threat. But the German infantry seemed to have lost interest in attacking over open ground. From their trenches in the Hanebeek valley they tried to sap forward, approaching under cover in a way reminiscent of eighteenth century sieges. The Buffs reported that the enemy infantry 'lacked push and determination'.

The losses in 1st Rifle Brigade mounted steeply. At one point, A Company was down to one officer and three men unwounded. These four, and some of the lightly wounded, fired rifles from the whole length of their trench section, trying to give the impression it was fully manned. They considered the German attack at 3 pm a rather feeble affair. At one stage Second Lieutenant Gibbs, Sergeant Vasselin and Rifleman Meredith ran forward and bombed the Germans out of one of the foremost saps. Though down to one man every 12 yards, the battalion held the line: 'We waited like this from 11 am to 8 pm and they never attacked. Goodness knows why. I think a good many people prayed pretty hard that day.' The official German account of the day stated: 'Again the attack had to come to a standstill, the troops whose strength had not been kept up, were at the end of their powers.' 51st Reserve Infantry Division reported that its infantry companies were down to about ninety men each. (That is less than half their full complement.)

At 11.45 pm Plumer issued the final orders for the 4,000-yard withdrawal that would see the British give up significant parts of the Salient: Shrewsbury Forest, Nonne Boschen and Polygon Woods, and Zonnebeke. All the artillery would be gone by 8.30 pm, half of the infantry by 9 pm, the remainder by 10.30 pm, and the final outpost line by midnight. Amazingly 3rd Monmouths found themselves forcing Belgian civilians to leave their farms, which they had been doggedly working through all the fighting and gas clouds going on around them.

When they were relieved that night, 1st Rifle Brigade had suffered 450 casualties. When the Buffs – now commanded by Captain Jackson – counted the cost they had lost nineteen officers and 702 men in a fortnight in the Salient. This broke down to six officers and sixty-seven men killed; nine officers and 259 wounded; two officers and thirteen men wounded and missing; two officers and 363 men missing. The extraordinarily high number of 'missing' reflects the fact that the losses fell heavily on the young draft that had joined the battalion on 1 May and whose names were not yet known to the battalion's record-keepers. The fighting was very severe in the general area of Berlin Wood. Two companies of 1st York and Lancaster and two companies of 5th King's Own were rushed up to give support; more followed as the fighting dragged on until 9 pm. Elements of 51st and 53rd Reserve Infantry Divisions were identified as the attackers. The Germans made large claims for their successes, issuing battle honours for places like Vanheule Farm that the British are quite sure they never lost.

A senior officer of 2nd Royal Dublin Fusiliers recorded an instance of the devotion to duty displayed by the BEF's young subalterns on this day, illustrating that intense 'cap badge' loyalty that was such an integral part of the performance of the British Army throughout its history:

> One of the many instances of unrecorded gallantry and determination to put 'the Regiment' first at all costs came to my notice in this action. Lieutenant J. R. F. Hall, a bright, energetic and fearless young lad, who had survived the tedious though strenuous winter existence in the trenches, was sent back from the front line with a party to bring up rations from near St Jean, just outside Ypres. When he reached the dump it was easy to see that he was greatly in need of even only a few hours' rest, and I got leave for him to remain for the night at the advanced Brigade Headquarters, and for somebody else to take the party back to the line. But I had done this without consulting Hall, who was furious when he heard of my action, and although almost exhausted from want of sleep and general overwork, pulled himself together and begged permission to be allowed to return with his party by saying – 'Now what's the use of being in a good regiment if you can't stick it?' He accordingly returned that night to the line in command of his men, and was killed during a gas attack in a later stage of the same action.

Later that night V Corps completed its withdrawal from the outer edge of the Salient without any further difficulty. Each front-line battalion sent two companies back at 9 pm. The last two companies went at 10.30 pm, but all left one or two rear parties, usually of some twenty or thirty men under a subaltern. These moved about the empty trenches, firing off shots at various places and generally simulating a normally held trench. They slipped away quietly around midnight. Some severely wounded men, with their RAMC attendants, were left behind to be gathered up by the Germans. Otherwise the trenches had been picked clean, every weapon, tool and piece of ammunition was carried away. Only one British soldier was reported missing, and he had fallen asleep in the trenches and sheepishly rejoined his unit at 6 am the following morning. The retirement from close contact with the enemy, in some places barely 50 yards, is an extremely hazardous operation of war, and the careful planning of Plumer's staff, and the discipline of his silent troops, reflected well on the BEF. The old Salient, 15 miles wide and 5 miles deep, had shrunk to 8 miles wide and 3 miles deep, requiring much fewer troops to hold it, and leaving less room to crowd vulnerable support units in behind the line. When 50th Division was able to get all its units back together, it found it had lost 122 officers and 3,624 other ranks in this tumultuous first battle – 472 killed, 1,996 wounded and 1,278 missing. When 3rd Royal Fusiliers finally pulled out for a rest they reckoned their losses so far at six officers and 100 men killed, and thirteen officers and 363 men wounded; 1st Hampshires counted six officers and 116 other ranks killed, five officers and 208 men wounded.

The Princess Pat's

One of the units falling back from Polygon Wood was the remarkable Princess Patricia's Canadian Light Infantry, about whom we shall hear a great deal more. When Canada put out the call for volunteers for a Canadian Expeditionary Force in 1914, the men were destined for battalions loosely based on the old militia system. The wealthy businessman, Alexander Hamilton Gault, proposed raising, at his own expense, a battalion entirely of men with previous military experience that would be available for immediate overseas service: 3,000 volunteers were interviewed by

Colonel Farquhar, who selected 1,098 officers and men, of whom 1,049 had served in the British armed forces (the others were eligible young men taken on as junior officers). Every regiment but one of the British Army was represented, along with the Royal Navy and Royal Marines. Half of them had seen active service, with a total of 771 campaign and service medals adorning their chests. Less than 10 per cent were native-born Canadians. Of the 'immigrants' 65 per cent were English, 15 per cent Scottish and 10 per cent Irish. The entire Edmonton Pipe Band had joined up together, as did the colourful 'Legion of Frontiersmen'. Colonel Farquhar was Military Secretary to the Duke of Connaught, then Governor-General of Canada. Through him the regiment was graced with the royal patronage of the Duke's daughter, Princess Patricia. This magnificent volunteer battalion was in England by 15 October 1914, was presented to the King on 4 November, and was assigned to 80th Brigade of 27th Division. They were in the trenches early in January 1915.

By 3 May they had completed a long tour of twelve days in the front line in Polygon Wood, a relatively quiet sector. Their relief by 2nd KSLI had been cancelled when that battalion was rushed into action elsewhere. They and their neighbours, 4th Rifle Brigade, had provided many working parties over several nights to prepare the fall-back position, and were dog tired as they began the perilous final withdrawal. The PPCLI left just three or four men to provide the last 'noisy' rearguard. They had lost about sixty men during the previous twelve days. As they filed into the new front line, where they appreciated the wire out in front but looked askance at the weak trenches, things were about to heat up.

'Selling the Hun a Dog'

As 3rd Monmouths put it, 'We evacuated our trench and "sold the Huns a dog"'. At dawn on 4 May the German artillery resumed its shelling of the now empty British front-line trenches, and 4th Division, under Major General Wilson, was able to reform intact for the first time in many days, with 2nd Canadian Brigade as their reserve. The rest of Alderson's Canadian Division was able to reorganise itself in the safety of the rear areas; their part in the battle was over. The new front line, some 3 miles from Ypres, was held by 27th Division on the right (from Hill 60 to the railway), by 28th Division in the centre, and by 4th Division on the left. A strong second line, well endowed with strongpoints, was being constructed behind them, and a third line was being built into the ramparts of Ypres and along the canal bank. There were plenty of gas alarms distributed along the new positions.

When the Germans finally realised the British were gone from the trenches before them they advanced very cautiously. Though they refer to a 'return to mobile warfare' they progressed very slowly through Polygon Wood and Zonnebeke, the ground littered with dead animals and birds. One German account of the forward move paints a sobering picture:

> The whole countryside is yellow, the battlefield is fearful. A curious, sour, heavy penetrating smell of dead bodies strikes one. Bodies of cows and pigs lie half decayed; splintered trees and stumps of avenues; shell crater after shell crater on the roads and in the fields.

Still the German General Balk was elated, feeling that the decisive breakthrough was at hand:

> There was again a scene of mobile warfare, which had not been witnessed for so long, as our leading lines in open order followed by close supports, broke onto the Flemish landscape. Long trains of artillery ammunition columns were brought up at a trot and reserves lay in green meadows and abandoned British positions. Everywhere in the devastated sector were the mighty results of our weapons to be seen.

When the infantry of XXVI and XXVII Reserve Corps bumped against what they thought were rearguards of British infantry around Frezenburg and Westhoek, they had, in fact, reached the forward zone of the new British line, and soon realised they would need more support to proceed further. The German artillery had to limber up and come forward to new gun positions, and when they resumed shelling later in the day they did great damage to the new trenches of 28th Division on the Frezenburg Ridge. Many of these had been hastily dug on forward-facing slopes and would be vulnerable to a very destructive fire over the next few days. The British soon found themselves digging new front-line trenches behind the rapidly disintegrating ones they had just fallen back to. The German infantry dug new trenches at distances varying from 200 to 600 yards from the British line.

'A Magnificent Spectacle'

It was about 6 am that the men of 4th Rifle Brigade saw the first German patrols. As the enemy deployed before 80th Brigade it was 'a magnificent spectacle'. His scouts were out in front as they came doubling forward under 'an indifferent fire'. It seems that some British infantry stood up in their trenches and cheered them on, in a curious – and perhaps last – display of chivalry towards a gallant foe. When the Germans deployed machine guns at 200 yards range everyone went to ground. Then the main force of German infantry appeared marching over Westhoek Ridge, with their officers mounted and directing movements. They made a wonderful target at 1,200 to 1,500 yards for the British artillery, but ammunition was so short that they were scarcely disturbed as they deployed into line and began to dig a solid trench line. The British had moved 122nd and 123rd Heavy Batteries RGA back into the Salient to provide some support, but they soon found themselves located and battered by the huge 430mm 'Big Bertha'. The Germans were all safely in place by 8 am, and their artillery had come into action from 7 am, suppressing the British infantry as the Germans dug in. It was a gruelling day for the troops of the PPCLI, who suffered 122 casualties in one day without any chance to retaliate. When relieved by 2nd KSLI at 10 pm they had been fourteen days in the line without a break.

This day saw the official decision to evacuate the remaining civilians from Ypres, to begin on 5 May, and which would take a few days to complete. With the town so battered and with large districts deserted it was sadly, but perhaps inevitably, subjected to frequent raids by parties of British soldiers who spent much of their free time 'liberating' items that took their fancy, be it military kit or 'souvenirs'.

'Hell let Loose'

As the British worked hard to improve their new lines, and the French maintained just enough activity on their front to pin the

German infantry in place, the Germans began to organise for a new gas attack when the conditions were favourable. Their infantry made a few probing attacks, easily fended off, but the German artillery took a relentless toll of the defenders. As the PPCLI staggered back past Hellfire Corner for a well-earned rest their Colonel, H. C. 'Teta' Buller, was hit by a shell splinter and would eventually lose an eye. Major Hamilton Gault, the founder of the regiment – just returned to duty from wounds received in a trench raid – found himself commanding 'his' battalion.

At one moment on 5 May 4th Rifle Brigade, in trenches along the forward edge of Sanctuary Wood, south of the Menin Road, saw some soldiers wearing British greatcoats 'trickling' towards them. Something suspicious about their demeanour alerted the Rifles to the fact that they were Germans wearing looted kit. They were driven off with rifle fire. Nevertheless 4th Rifle Brigade found themselves overlooked by the enemy at some 600 yards range and endured heavy and accurate shelling that cost them 150 killed and 250 wounded in two days.

Now 3rd Monmouths found themselves being split up and sent out by company to wherever they were needed: C Company went to help 2nd East Yorkshires just south of the Ypres–Frezenburg Road. They found the trenches full of gassed men, and that evening they had to bury many of the dead just behind the parados. Their company commander, Captain Steel, was a medical doctor in civilian life and performed wonderful acts of courage and salvation in addition to his normal duties as an infantry officer. One company of East Yorkshires was down to twenty men, so their assistance was timely, and 3rd Monmouths' A Company was sent to 5th King's Own. Sergeant Davies left this record:

On Wednesday morning the 'fun' started quite early and the Germans sent all sorts of stuff at us. It simply rained shells, and about midday we were called out to try and reinforce the King's Own Regiment, who had suffered badly. We set out, a platoon at a time, under Captain R. A. Lewis, but the trenches were in such a bad position that we had to go over a ridge to get to them, in full view of the German lines, so you can just guess they let our boys have it hot. Nearly half the platoon was cut down, including Captain Lewis, and it was a forlorn hope, so the order was given to retire, which we did until dusk.

Private Barry was in the same company: 'Talk about hell let loose – it was worse than that – and for the whole day we were lying on our faces and hands in the bottom of the trenches not daring to move.' B Company went to the right of the line to help 1st York and Lancasters, finding themselves next to the PPCLI. They were not impressed to find the trench line following a row of poplar trees – a perfect target for the German gunners. The fourth company of the battalion remained in the GHQ Line as a reserve.

The point where the new front line joined up with the old line, on the eastern outskirts of Armagh Wood, was held by 1st Leinsters. At 9 am they may have been subjected to a gas attack, or caught some of the gas released at Hill 60, but were not too badly affected. All the men had pads to cover their mouth and most remembered to breathe in through their mouth and out through their nose. Inevitably, in the heat of battle, some men instinctively breathed through their nose and fell victim to the poison gas. A violent attack ensued and some popular officers died in the fighting, as recorded in the diary of a Leinsterman:

> Our brave Captain G. Adams and Second Lieutenant Kahn took up rifles and fixed bayonets and fired with us fetching down man after man. I saw a German officer step out of a wood and in less than one minute a shell came and brave Captain Adams and Second Lieutenant Kahn and two men were killed instantly by the same shell, both men and officers lying in a heap, and his guide and servant was struck by the same shell and severely wounded. It was awful, this was in the same trench as us and on my left a shell came and killed three more and wounded about six more . . .

Their Transport Officer, Lieutenant Westmacott, who could have passed the battle safely in the rear, had begged to be allowed to do the normal work of an infantry officer in the trenches because of the shortage of experienced officers. He was helping an officer from an incoming relief battalion to erect a wire entanglement when both were killed. The battalion lost three officers and twenty-seven men killed, and two officers and 100 men wounded in this 'small affair'.

Campaign Chronicle

The Loss of Hill 60

The big reverse for the British on 5 May was the final loss of Hill 60. On this tortured hill, described as 'a mere rubbish heap of mangled trenches and craters', an enlarged 15th Brigade was in place: 1st Norfolks, 2nd Duke of Wellingtons and 1st Bedfords were on the hill; 1st Dorsets in close support; 1st Cheshires and 6th King's were in reserve. Major Cowie of the Dorsets was the senior field officer in the sector, with overall responsibility for its defence. At 5.45 am he was just returning from the front line when he was hit by a shell fragment. This much-liked officer died of his wounds some two weeks later.

At 8.45 am, without the 'normal' accompaniment of a preliminary bombardment, a gas cloud was released against the Dukes. By a cruel fluke the wind blew in just such a way that the gas cloud drifted not across the trench but along its whole length. Thus the carefully planned gambit to move away from the front of the gas cloud to the extremities of the trench, leaving the reserves to counter-attack and restore the line, didn't work. Instead it crowded the men in parts of the trench greatly affected by gas. The gas hung very heavily in the trenches and only a well-soaked respirator would work against it. Most of the defenders succumbed. Certainly the Germans had captured the whole front-line trench within fifteen minutes.

CSM Shephard, 1st Dorsets, saw it all and was harshly, and unfairly, critical of 2nd Duke's, who bore the brunt of the attack and losses.

> We received no definite order to reinforce, but seeing the Wellingtons running down the railway we started on our own. How we got up I can hardly tell. The enemy (of course expecting the troops to retire) shelled heavily with shrapnel to catch them. The communicating trench was almost choked with Dukes, some very bad, others unaffected.

They saw the Germans swarming over Hill 60, so they took post in the support trenches and made sure 'Jerry' got no further. They inflicted heavy losses on the enemy but couldn't stop them infiltrating around their flanks. The Cheshires joined them and the line was restored. Their popular, scholarly CO, Lieutenant Colonel

Scott, was to have taken command of the sector but was killed before he ever got to the hill. Major Hughes took command of the battalion. The four machine guns lost by the Dukes on the hill were turned against the Dorsets and Cheshires to their great annoyance. The German artillery had, as usual, extended its field of fire to fall heavily on the reverse slopes and support lines, crashing amongst the fleeing defenders and any reinforcements trying to make their way forward. It did not help that shells from a British 4.5-inch howitzer battery were falling on those Dorsets clinging to the support line. Young Mansel-Pleydell took command of his company after Captain Lilly was wounded in the arm by that British gunfire. They quickly organised trench blocks and savagely assailed with the bayonet any Germans found in the lines. They were looking for revenge and it was a very unfortunate German to be found by them that day. (Mansel-Pleydell would be promoted to command his A Company, and would die in May 1916 patrolling No Man's Land near Thiepval in preparation for the Somme offensive.)

Another gas cloud was released at 11 am, hitting the Bedfords to the north-east of the hill. More battalions were fed into the fight to stop the enemy advancing further. To add to the defenders' misery at about 1 pm the British artillery, having been told the Germans had got into the support line, began shelling the very trenches held by British infantry. CSM Shephard recorded the desperate state of affairs:

> We tried to telephone them but [the] wires [were] broken, so we had to endure it. It was a perfect Hell, shelled from front and by our own artillery in rear. The enemy's bombs, rifle fire etc., the fear of more gas. Were ever human beings asked to endure such as this before? We were of course hourly expecting to be relieved. We were all exhausted. I had a strong dose of gas, but managed to vomit in time.

Reinforcements arrived from King's Own Scottish Borderers and Royal West Kents, from O'Gowan's 13th Brigade. Despite another small release of gas around 7 pm, to no great effect, 13th Brigade was ordered to counter-attack and reclaim Hill 60. After a hastily arranged bombardment from 10 pm to 10.20 pm the attack went in, from exactly the same trenches as they had launched from on 17 April, and failed. It seems that some of the infantry ran into the bombardment, which went on longer on some parts of the hill than others. After some two or three hours of fighting the attackers were driven back by the increasing levels of enfilade fire coming from beyond the railway cutting.

When the Dorsets were relieved that night they were down to 165 unwounded men – all that was left from a battalion strength of 800 one week before; the Dukes, who started the battle with 500 men, were down to 150. It would be 7 June 1917 before the British recaptured Hill 60 in the great operation that took the whole of the Messines Ridge. It was a brutally realistic assessment that suggested that 'the men were either tired out or raw, and the dash of the April attack was absent'. There was a certain bitterness in the KOSB history as it made this conclusion about the struggle for Hill 60:

> It is somewhat of an enigma that Hill 60 was considered worth 100 officers and 3,000 Other Ranks of 5th Division. Its loss on 5th May, after being an undesirable British possession in which to be quartered for three weeks, had no appreciable effect on the Western Theatre . . . No attempt is made in the Official History to link the episode to some strategic scheme . . . Mr Buchan thinks that Hollebeke would have been untenable if we had retained Hill 60. Be it so.

Elsewhere in the Salient the British infantry had to endure a steady and relentless shelling, with both high-explosive and gas shells. Casualty lists mounted remorselessly and battle strength leeched away. The 2nd East Yorkshires (83rd Brigade) endured a three-hour bombardment, including gas shells, and then drove off a German infantry attack, forcing the enemy to dig in still 300 yards away from the British lines. The fight cost the battalion ten officers wounded, thirty-five men killed, 134 wounded and six missing. The 2nd KSLI would lose twenty-nine killed, and an officer and thirty-two men wounded on 5 May, another thirty killed and wounded on the 6th, and, even when relieved and pulled back to work on repairing the GHQ Line, another twelve lost on the 7th.

"Orace, You're for 'Ome' (Apocryphal greeting of 'Wully' Robertson to Smith-Dorrien)

The day of 6 May passed relatively quietly, always excepting the persistent shelling by German artillery, and even that seemed a little lighter. In the early hours an attempt by German marine infantry at a surprise attack on Mouse Trap Farm, assisted by heavy howitzer fire, was defeated. In this fierce little battle 2nd Northumberland Fusiliers had the curious 'butcher's bill' of just one second lieutenant and two sergeants killed, and no other injuries at all.

The day is significant for General Smith-Dorrien, not unreasonably, writing to Sir John French asking for his position and role to be clarified, a previous letter of 1 May having been totally ignored. In his memoirs Smith-Dorrien, carefully eschewing any accusation of laying blame, says he realised that it was the commander of Second Army, not the Army itself, that had fallen from favour with the Commander-in-Chief. His letter was typically thoughtful, and full of concern for the fighting efficiency of Second Army:

> I have just received an order for Army commanders to meet at your house at 9 am tomorrow. I am still in ignorance of the action you intend to take regarding the papers, so important to me and the Army I command, I sent you on the 1st instant, and it would make things easier for me, were I to know your views before the meeting.
>
> Whatever may be the reason, there can be no question that your attitude to me for some time past has tended to show that you had, for some reason or other unknown to me, ceased to trust me.
>
> Latterly I have been shorn first of one wing of my Army, and then of the other, on the latter occasion the announcement being made in such a way and in such terms, as to leave no doubt in the minds of many in the Second Army that their Commander was no longer believed in by their Chief.
>
> My position as Army Commander has become impossible, and I regard my remaining in command with a cloud hanging over me ready to burst at any moment, as a positive

danger to the cause for which we are fighting.

Plenty of complicated situations have arisen in the last few months, and the difficulty of dealing with them has been greatly enhanced by the knowledge that unless I was successful, I and the Second Army would be blamed – in fact, I have had more to fear from the rear than from the front.

We have got to win this war, and to do so there must be no weak links in the chain. Your attitude to me constitutes a very seriously weak link, and I feel sure that, trying as that attitude has been to me, you have not wished to carry it quite so far as to appoint someone else to command Second Army in my place.

This step is, however, the only one which to my mind will strengthen up the chain again, and it is to render it more easy for you to take it without further delay that I am writing this letter.

Please do not let any false considerations for me personally stand in the way, for the War Office will doubtless find some place for me where I can still do useful work towards helping our Army fighting in France.

Yours sincerely

H. L. Smith-Dorrien

He received the brutally short order to hand over his whole command to Plumer and return to England forthwith. No reason was ever given. The soldiers in the Salient instinctively knew this was an injustice. 'Before he left for England, Smith-Dorrien was amply justified by the withdrawal taking place' is just one typical remark made by witnesses to the events.

*

So, from 7 May 1915, Plumer became GOC Second Army, a post he would hold – with one short intermission for service in Italy in 1917–1918 – until the end of the war. He was 'The Guardian of the Salient' for the rest of his time on the Western Front.

The last flicker of fighting in this phase of the battle involved another German failure at Mouse Trap Farm, and a last try at

Hill 60 by Britain's 5th Division. At 2.30 am Lieutenant Colonel Withycombe and his company commanders made a front-line reconnaissance of the Zwartelen Salient just to the west of the hill. At dawn King's Own Yorkshire Light Infantry, and bombing platoons of 2nd Royal Irish Rifles and the Cheshires, attacked in vain. The Cheshires' attempt to break into the enemy position by clearing a trench block failed and this left two weak companies of the KOYLI committed to the attack. The leading waves were lost entirely, all the men being killed or captured. Some appeared to have entered the enemy trenches and so a third company was sent over. Perhaps fortunately, the fourth company lost direction and ended up in the trenches occupied by the Cheshires. When they were relieved that night 2nd KOYLI had lost eleven officers and 177 men that day. The long ordeal of 5th Division in this sector had cost them 100 officers and 3,000 other ranks.

Later in the day German infantry was seen to mass near the Menin Road on the front of 81st Brigade. The British artillery was able to get onto the target, dispersing the enemy before any attack developed. The night was described as 'noisy', with lots of red flares being fired, with intermittent rifle and machine-gun fire.

After just two days' rest the PPCLI were back in the line to relieve the KSLI on the Bellewaarde Ridge north of Hooge. With a new draft of men the battalion numbered fourteen officers and 600 other ranks. The line had been improved a little but it was impossible to move about in daylight without attracting a torrent of fire, and there was still no connection between the two companies in the front line and the two in the support line just behind them. They arrived just in time to face the next great German offensive.

8 May: Victory at Hand?

Understandably, Duke Albrecht was keen to follow up the success of having forced a considerable British retreat and having recaptured Hill 60. He had spent four days organising his Fourth Army for another major attack. He moved his heavy artillery closer to the front held by 27th and 28th Divisions, between the Menin Road and the Frezenburg Ridge. He deployed XXVI and XXVII Reserve

Corps, and XV Corps, together with 37th and 38th Landwehr Brigades, 2nd Reserve Ersatz Brigade and 4th Marine Brigade. While these were all veteran formations, they were also the same units that had been attacking since 22 April. Many of their best-trained men had fallen; the ranks were full of draft replacements. Still the reports suggested the men were keen to make one more big effort to smash the British and seize Ypres once and for all.

The new British line was vulnerable in places. On the right 27th Division was largely sheltered in wooded country. In the centre 28th Division had part of its line on a reverse slope, but from Frezenburg village to Mouse Trap Farm their new trenches were on a forward slope, under complete observation from the German lines. This positioning was necessary to provide useful forward observation for the defending artillery. The new trenches were far from complete. They were narrow and only some 3 feet deep, because of the high water table. They were built up with sandbag barricades, hopelessly vulnerable to artillery bombardment. There were no adequate dug-outs or communication trenches back to the support line. This position – far from satisfactory in an ideal world – had to be retained, as the next defensible position was over half a mile further back, dangerously close to Ypres itself. On the left, 4th Division held stronger lines from Mouse Trap Farm to the canal, resting largely on reverse slopes.

The GHQ Line was a solid barrier, and behind it work was progressing on the 'Canal Line'. With typical care Plumer had even instituted work on a defensive line to the west of Ypres. He knew that the Allies would begin their spring offensives the next day (with the British attacking at Aubers Ridge) and ordered a 'tenacious defence' to pin the enemy to the Salient. Second Army was left very weak in heavy artillery, with only six 60-pounder and twelve outmoded 4.7-inch guns to face the overwhelming enemy superiority in artillery.

'Hell with the Lid off'

The 8th of May was to be an extraordinary, and critical, day. During the night enemy patrols had been active and German marines had assaulted 2nd Northumberland Fusiliers at Mouse Trap Farm. The attackers had been bloodily repulsed.

But at 5.30 am a violent bombardment of the whole British front

Duke Albrecht of Württemberg (1865–1939)

Born in 1865 in Vienna, Albrecht entered the German Army in 1883, being commissioned into the Lancers or 'Uhlan' branch of the cavalry. He progressed through the ranks to Colonel-General, commanding the Sixth Army Inspectorate based at Stuttgart. He was Colonel-in-Chief of 119th Grenadier Regiment.

In 1914 he commanded the Fourth German Army of five Prussian corps, fighting first in the Ardennes and then on the Marne. His reconstituted Fourth Army, now of one veteran and four reserve corps, moved up to the Yser and Ypres fronts. He delivered some of the bloody assaults in which the young volunteers of the Reserve Corps were slaughtered in the 'Kindermord' of 1914. In 1915 he conducted the attacks on the Ypres Salient that introduced gas warfare onto the scene. Later that year he, along with other royal army commanders, was awarded the *Pour le Mérite* for the defence of the West. In 1916 he was promoted to *Generalfeldmarschall*. From 1917 to 1918 he was commander of Army Group Albrecht that covered the 'quiet' southern end of the Western Front.

He could have succeeded to the throne of Württemberg in 1918 but the title was swept away in the republican reforms of the day. In 1921 he retired to his castle and, avoiding political entanglements, died in 1939.

He was a thorough, professional soldier in the Prussian mould, always well served by competent Chiefs of Staff. At Second Ypres he had to fight only with the troops to hand, assisted by the gas weapon, and put the Allies under a great deal of pressure, inflicting far heavier casualties than he suffered.

began to develop, which rose to a crescendo between 7 and 9 am. In its exposed forward slope trenches 83rd Brigade took the brunt of it. Losses among 3rd Monmouths, 1st King's Own Yorkshire Light Infantry and 2nd King's Own began to mount sharply. From 7 am the shelling between the Menin Road and Mouse Trap Farm intensified, falling heavily on 80th, 83rd, 84th and part of 12th

Brigades. Even the German field artillery was firing high-explosive shell. The British artillery had not one round of HE with which to retaliate. They were wholly confined to firing shrapnel rounds. For two hours the British front trenches were systematically demolished. From 8.30 am the German bombardment extended to the support lines and all roads leading to the battle area.

Yet when the German infantry assault came in at 8.30 am, striking the lines of 3rd Monmouths, 2nd King's Own, 1st Suffolks and 2nd Cheshires, the steady British infantry drove them off. With typical bravado a man of 3rd Monmouths recalled, 'We were only a handful of men, and they came on in thousands, but we kept them at bay.' A second attack, delivered at 9 am with renewed artillery preparation, was also defeated. But the losses amongst the defenders were grievous and nothing could get up through the German barrage, which, having thoroughly pulverised the front trenches, had switched to the supports and reverse slopes to cut off any supplies and reinforcements trying to get to the beleaguered front.

83rd Brigade Collapses

So, when the third attack was delivered at 10 am on either side of Frezenburg village, the German infantry finally stormed the front line of 83rd Brigade. The attackers did not have an easy time of it:

> After they had finished with our fire trench they came on, thinking they had us beaten completely, but there was a company of men in the support trenches and when Mr Fritz came over the ridge he found another trench about 500 yards away. The boys in the support had had more sleep than those in the fire trench and had not been subjected to such severe shelling, and they soon showed Fritz what a rifle, when handled properly, could do.

It was a time of maximum confusion. The King's Own were overwhelmed and very few escaped; 2nd East Yorks were trying to reinforce the line as other battalions were being given the option to retire; 3rd Monmouths had just received an order to fall back 400 yards to the support line and Colonel Gough was actually organising a local counter-attack to free them from the position. Some thought they had been authorised to fall back to the GHQ

Line; others said the message was 'All for yourselves.' In the confused fighting they had to make their escape as best they could. Private William Millie was a Royal Engineers signalman attached to 3rd Monmouths:

> So I grabbed my bandolier, rifle and telephone and made my way back to the barbed wire, which was not far away. I could not find the opening so the only thing I could do was to cut my way underneath. Luckily I got me [sic] pliers with me. I got through all right. Some way back there was an officer with a revolver stopping people. 'Who are you? Who are you?' Things were all any how, all in daylight of course. I told him I was 1/3rd Monmouths and asked, 'Do you know where they are?' He said, 'No!' There was [sic] a lot of wires about so I tapped into them and couldn't get anybody, couldn't even get Brigade.

This was the moment the German commanders had waited for and the attack was pressed home along the entire front from the Menin Road to Mouse Trap Farm. But now, as the German infantry surged up over the crest of the ridge, it was their turn to feel the full weight of British defensive fire. This was exactly the target that shrapnel shells were designed for and the German infantry paid a heavy price for their success. Soon all forward movement ceased and they concentrated on expanding the gap they had created, fighting their way along the trench system; 1st KOYLI on the right, and the Monmouths and King's Own on the left were thrust aside bodily. Two companies of KOYLI and one of Monmouths hung on a little longer than most to try to stem the tide, but to no avail. All four of KOYLI's machine guns were wrecked or buried by shellfire. Captain Mallinson commanded the battalion after all the field officers were hit. When the PPCLI on their right fell back, B Company 3rd Monmouths could claim to be the most forward unit of the British Army in the Salient, if not for very long. The RAMC dressing station at Verlorenhoek was almost overrun. It was on fire and the medical staff evacuated it, and were reduced to treating the wounded as they lay in the road alongside.

The British were, of course, directing reserves towards the critical point: 2nd East Yorkshires were ordered forward to assist 3rd Monmouths, and half of 85th Brigade was placed under 83rd

Brigade's control. Brigadier General Boyles (83rd Brigade) belatedly realised how bad things were, having received news from wounded officers returning from the front lines, and tried to stop the East Yorkshires. Only seven officers and 221 men strong, the battalion had already manfully set about their task. In a welter of confused messages, and under heavy enemy fire, these troops were caught up in the retirement of the King's Own and Monmouths. When 5th King's Own came up from brigade reserve they were joined by the determined men of the East Yorkshires, and together, barely 550 strong, they advanced under fire for some 1,000 yards before being forced to fall back to their start line, the GHQ Line. While not affecting the battle in a decisive way, they certainly contributed to the confusion and eventual discomfort of the enemy. 83rd Brigade was exhausted, mustering barely 600 men – 1st KOYLI had lost ten officers and 417 other ranks; 3rd Monmouths were down to four officers and 130 men – they had 259 killed in one day and some 400 wounded, making this one of the heaviest losses for any one battalion at Second Ypres; 2nd King's Own were down to four officers and ninety-four men.

The 'Stonewall' Brigade

On the right of 83rd Brigade, two battalions of 80th Brigade clung desperately to the front line. 4th King's Royal Rifle Corps and Princess Patricia's Canadian Light Infantry were holding Hooge Wood and Bellewaarde Ridge. Soon after dawn the German bombardment had begun, joined by their heavy guns from 7 am. The front line was systematically obliterated; machine-gun posts were wrecked or buried; the wire was blown away. Every man was pushed up into the firing line – all the cooks, pioneers and officers' servants. At 8 am Hamilton Gault sent off a message to brigade headquarters, warning that a major attack must develop soon. A sudden burst of intense machine-gun fire, clearly designed to force the defenders down in their trenches, heralded the assault by 54th Reserve Infantry Division. The first rush was broken up by rifle fire. Only some eighty to 100 Germans made it to a hedgerow and some ruined buildings just in front of the PPCLI line. Rifle fire alone forced the Germans along the hedgerow to beat a retreat, crawling back across No Man's Land.

The front battalions were joined by 2nd King's Shropshire

Light Infantry and 4th Rifle Brigade. The KSLI had their colonel, J. R. Bridgford, wounded, ten men killed and twenty-seven wounded as they struggled to form a flank guard facing north. One of their companies was commanded by their transport officer, so short were they of infantry officers. He died of wounds received in this fight. Then German infantry seized a commanding piece of ground just in front of the British line, unoccupied because it would have formed too pronounced a salient, and successfully brought up machine guns. They built up such a level of fire that the PPCLI had to begin abandoning the front line and falling back into their support trench. At 9 am eyewitnesses reported: 'There seemed to be an astounding silence with just an occasional rifle shot, and then we realised that the German infantry were upon us.' A mass of Germans swept up to the front line, shouting loud words of encouragement to each other. On the left, No. 2 Company stopped them cold, but they poured into the trenches of No. 1 Company, and developed their attack along the trench. The PPCLI saw a puzzling line of small white flags go up all along the lost front line. Unfortunately this was not a sign of willingness to surrender, but the German infantry putting up markers of the line reached for their artillery observers. At once the German guns lifted and fire crashed down on the support line and the area behind it. Major Hamilton Gault was wounded twice in quick succession and had to hand over command to Captain Adamson. No. 1 Company fell back to the supports, covered by Captain Dennison, Lieutenant Lane and a handful of men. Neither of these officers were ever seen again and few of their men escaped. No. 2 Company ran out of ammunition and had to abandon their part of the front line. Finding the small communication trench blown in, they had to go up over the open ground and lost very heavily indeed. Several men went to ground and kept up a sniping duel with the encroaching Germans. By 10 am the whole of the front line was lost. Major John Harington of 4th Rifle Brigade personally checked the situation in the supports and reported: 'P.P. have suffered 75 per cent casualties and the position is critical. Reinforcements badly wanted at once. All my battalion is up.'

As 4th Rifle Brigade arrived to take some of the pressure off the Princess Patricia's, Captain Adamson – already badly wounded –

directed their machine-gun section into the trenches to assist in beating off renewed German attacks around 10 am. Under heavy bombardment the Canadians' strength dwindled to barely 150 men and the whole of 4th Rifle Brigade was moved up to help. One Canadian wrote home, 'We have seen the Angels today. They had R.B. on their shoulders, and the biggest of the Angels were those who bore the machine guns on their shoulders too'. German flank attacks were defeated, though D Company, 4th RB, on the right, shrank from sixty riflemen to just four unwounded in the course of the fight. C Company saw some Germans digging in a bit too close for comfort and charged them with the bayonet, putting them to flight.

Though they had lost touch with 83rd Brigade, which was being driven back nearly a mile towards Potijze and Verlorenhoek, 80th Brigade managed to extend its lines to cover the flanks of the breach and the main line held firm. Fortunately the Germans did not extend their attack south of this point and 27th Division was quite secure. 81st Brigade was able to send up 1st Argyll and Sutherland Highlanders and half of 9th Argylls to bolster the flank guards. Well might Major General Snow later write: 'He is proud to have command of a Division which includes such a "stonewall" brigade as the 80th have proved themselves to be.'

The crisis of the day's fight was from 10 am to 2 pm as the brigade clung on under unceasing bombardment, machine-gun fire and infantry attacks. Machine guns were repeatedly knocked out of place, buried and remounted. One was unearthed three times before all its crew were killed. Corporal Dover of the PPCLI fired his machine gun until it literally exploded in his hands. Terribly wounded, he was picked up by stretcher-bearers, only to be killed by a sniper as he was being carried to the rear. As officer losses mounted, the NCOs and senior privates took on their share of responsibility for keeping the line intact. RSM Fraser, one of the first PPCLI volunteers, was killed as he stood on the parados handing out ammunition and directing fire. Only four lieutenants and the wounded Captain Adamson remained with the PPCLI as their battalion losses topped 80 per cent. No wounded could be got away from the trenches and the conditions deteriorated rapidly. Around midday ammunition ran very low and it was nearly 3 pm before a platoon of the KSLI got through with a good supply of .303 bullets. This coincided with a slight easing of the pressure on 80th Brigade. One last German rush was shot down and the battle began to wind down. Observers to the rear remarked how little there was of unwounded men 'straggling' to the rear during the tremendous fight.

From 5 pm the German gunfire became 'desultory' and the crisis passed on this part of the line. When the PPCLI was relieved by 3rd KRRC at 11.30 pm Captain Adamson was already in hospital and the battalion was led away by Lieutenant Niven and numbered barely 150. As they marched away men of 80th Brigade cheered them in recognition of their great effort. They had suffered grievous losses amongst their 'originals', including the deaths of twenty-one sergeants.

One of the Great Tragedies of the War

Over on the far left flank another critical moment developed. 84th Brigade was caught up in the German attack and their flank was exposed when 83rd Brigade was forced back. They were able to extend a flank guard to cover the breach and 2nd Cheshires, 1st Monmouths and 2nd Northumberland Fusiliers held the front line, under heavy fire and with mounting losses. Probing attacks by German infantry were driven off. At 11.15 am 12th Londons (The Rangers) were ordered forward from brigade reserve. After all the fighting they had seen since 24 April the Rangers were barely 200 strong. As they set off from the GHQ Line they were forced to bunch up as they passed through gaps in the wire. They came under fire immediately and, in one of the great tragedies of the war, the battalion melted away under artillery and machine-gun fire as it approached the line of 1st Monmouths. All thirteen officers fell. That night they were commanded by a sergeant (W. J. Hornall), and comprised just fifty-three men, mostly pioneers and signallers. The one machine gun they managed to bring forward was put in place but the crew were soon all killed or wounded. An officer of the Monmouths kept it in action in a useful role, covering their exposed flank, until the gun was itself destroyed. It would be many months before the battalion was rebuilt and returned to the BEF's Order of Battle.

As the British line crumbled under the relentless pressure, German infantry found gaps into which they could penetrate and start to roll up the line along the trenches; 2nd Cheshires were the first to break at around 1 pm. Their headquarters was stormed and their commander killed; the three forward companies were overwhelmed, losing thirteen officers and 382 men. Only about 100 men, under two second lieutenants, managed to scamper back to the GHQ Line. Next the Suffolks were completely surrounded, losing twelve officers and 432 men. Only one officer and twenty-nine men escaped to the rear. Colonel Wallace distributed a box of very fine Havana cigars amongst his men rather than see them taken by the Germans. But he and all the men around him, sheltering together in a shell hole, were soon rounded up and captured by the enemy. Private Crask, MM, remembers that the Germans were full of confidence, certain that they would soon be in Ypres, with Calais and London next on their list of conquests. The Germans were attentive to their prisoners and Crask thought they were Hanoverians of 77th Infantry Regiment. This regiment does not appear on the German Order of Battle for Second Ypres and is one more example of British prisoners claiming to be with 'friendly' Hanoverians.

Soon 1st Monmouths found themselves assailed in flank and rear. They got a message to 2nd Northumberland Fusiliers, warning them that they couldn't hold on and were going to try to fall back, maintaining a flank guard. In the attempt the battalion was swamped by attackers and destroyed. Their commander and second-in-command were both killed. Only two officers and 120 men answered the evening roll call. 84th Brigade, with six battalions under command, barely mustered 1,400 men at 5 pm.

A Two-Mile Gap

By the early afternoon there was a 2-mile gap torn in the British front line, with the line holding firm on either side of it. On the left 12th Brigade, of 4th Division, firmly repelled an attack on its line, and 27th Division was little troubled on the right. The Germans just did not have enough in reserve to extend the attack further. The RFC confirmed that there was no movement in the German rear, indicating there were no reserves on hand to reinforce their early success.

Now 85th Brigade was to be the centrepiece in a counter-attack designed to recover all the lost ground. Two battalions had reached Potijze and were ordered at 2.40 pm to prepare themselves for the attack – 3rd Middlesex, with 500 men to hand, and 1st York and Lancasters, newly reinforced to an impressive 950 strong (about one-third of whom were recent drafts). By 4 pm 2nd East Surreys (85th Brigade) had joined them, together with the remnants of 2nd East Yorks and 2nd and 5th King's Own. By 5 pm 85th Brigade was complete, when 3rd Royal Fusiliers arrived. The East Surreys said they attacked 'off the march', meaning they had no time to rest, or reorganise or reconnoitre, after they arrived.

The Germans had begun to dig in, and site their machine guns, precisely because they expected just such a hurried counter-attack. As the British infantry moved forward, with orders simply to 'push on and occupy our old trenches', they were in plain view and were shelled remorselessly by the German artillery. Apart from linking up with 80th Brigade on the right, the attack failed completely, never really threatening the new German line at any point. A splendid brigade was effectively annihilated with nothing to show for it: 1st York and Lancasters had their colonel killed and had shrunk from nearly 1,000 men to eighty-three, under a sergeant; 3rd Middlesex were down to 289, having lost six officers and 383 other ranks – most of their platoons were commanded by lance-corporals; 2nd East Surreys were down to eight officers and thirty men; 2nd East Yorkshires to three officers and 200 men; 5th King's Own to a sad total of ninety-one riflemen.

While this tragedy unfolded, 2nd Northumberland Fusiliers, despite their flank being turned by the destruction of 1st Monmouths, continued to hold their front line. When we say they were supported by 1st Welch, that proud battalion was barely the strength of one company. The Fusiliers were given the option to retire to the GHQ Line but were so successful in beating off the German infantry that they elected to stay where they were. Just as they were considering a withdrawal, the German infantry were seen to launch an attack that crashed into the battalion's stretcher-bearers, and onto the wounded men moving away to the rear. In furious indignation the Fusiliers poured fire into the attackers and drove them off. Lieutenant Colonel Enderby had gone into the forward fire trench at 6.15 pm to begin the organisation for a possible withdrawal. He was trapped there when a German bombardment of great violence crashed down around him. It stopped suddenly and, on a flare signal, German infantry flooded forward and completed the destruction of 1st Monmouths on the right. The Northumberland Fusiliers were now surrounded on three sides, and the headquarters of B, C and D companies were stormed. Colonel Enderby was wounded and captured in the fighting, as was his Adjutant, Captain Auld. Auld had been delivering orders to a part of the front line and found himself trapped in a fire bay with one stretcher-bearer. German infantry burst in and bayoneted the unarmed private and would have killed Auld but a German sergeant major cried out: 'Nein, nein! Das ist der Kommandant.' One platoon of A Company was destroyed but the last three platoons on the far left of the line, in a strong position just east of Mouse Trap Farm and somewhat less battered than other posts, fought on like demons. The immensely strong Captain Hart inspired the defence. When a German officer called for their surrender, Hart shot him dead with his revolver. He was killed soon after, and Second Lieutenant Watson took command. The only other officer present, Second Lieutenant Lord, was badly wounded. Sergeants took over the command of the platoons; individual privates behaved with matchless determination, even counter-attacking with bombs on one occasion. One soldier 'borrowed' a machine gun from a neighbouring unit, carrying it 40 yards over open ground, and firing it until it was wrecked beyond use.

At nightfall the Germans gave up their costly attacks. A badly wounded Second Lieutenant Watson had just sixty-five men left in the front line, a stand that can truly be described as heroic. When relieved by 1st East Lancashires (at 4 am the next morning), the survivors were joined by all that was left of the other three companies – two second lieutenants and fifty-one other ranks. The battalion recorded six officers and twelve men known to be killed; three officers and 126 men wounded; five officers and 284 men missing. Of these latter, eighty were later identified as prisoners of war, and so another 209 were added to the number killed. The Transport Officer, Captain Stephen, commanded the battalion as it was rebuilt with new drafts. When it reached nine officers (eight of them brand-new second lieutenants) and 457 men, it was considered ready to return to the line.

Lieutenant Colonel Enderby later recalled his first interview as a prisoner. He was graciously received, and the German commander said, 'But why look so depressed about it all?' Enderby said the almost complete annihilation of his battalion was sufficient excuse. The German general replied, 'Maybe so. But you may reflect that had it not been for the resistance of that battalion I should not now be here. I should have been in Ypres tonight.'

Victory Snatched From the Jaws of Defeat

However, the day took an extraordinary turn. Major General Bulfin had made an appeal to 4th Division for help to shore up his collapsing line. After the local reserves had been used up, 10th Brigade was ordered forward, at about 1.30 pm, from its camps west of the canal. They did not arrive in the GHQ Line until 7.30 pm, too late for a major attack. They were simply asked to deploy in front of the British barbed wire in front of Mouse Trap Farm and make a minor forward movement to 'tidy up' the line. Perhaps because it came so soon after the failed effort of 85th Brigade, this small advance (by 1st Royal Warwickshires, 1st Royal Irish Fusiliers and 2nd Royal Dublin Fusiliers) became the decisive intervention in the day's battle. The German defenders of Hill 33, east of Wieltje, bolted and their flight caused a general withdrawal of large elements of XXVI and XXVII Reserve Corps. The entire German Fourth Army went over to the defensive, making no major attack for the next five days. Clearly the Germans had exhausted themselves by their persistent attacks, and it is at precisely such delicate moments that the actions of a formed body of troops can have results out of all proportion to their numbers. Curiously, the unit history of 2nd Royal Dublin Fusiliers published in 1923 seems to be entirely unaware of the importance of this action. The Official History, published in 1927, took full cognisance of the German war histories and was able to put this remarkable event in context.

The British were able to form a new line to seal off the 2-mile breach in their front. It ran behind the Verlorenhoek Ridge, some three-quarters of a mile behind the original front. The ground lost had been the most exposed and vulnerable part of the line, and the line was the better for it. Both 27th and 28th Divisions were ordered to make new counter-attacks later that evening, but the battalion commanders all refused to countenance such folly. It was too dark, the situation too confused, and the orders were officially cancelled.

British losses had been terrible. Eleven battalion commanders, leading from the front, had become casualties. The old battalions of the Regular Army were further depleted of trained officers, NCOs and men; their ranks were full of new drafts now. Even units in the reserve positions suffered from the shelling: 1st Hampshires (11th Brigade) at Wieltje Farm lost their celebrated commander, Lieutenant Colonel Hicks. He had served with the battalion for twenty-five years, and commanded it for six months, but did not survive the complications that set in after his right leg was amputated. The Germans reported the capture of 800 British prisoners in the period 1 to 8 May, most of which must have been taken in the course of the confused fighting of 8 May. Allenby, now commanding V Corps in place of Plumer, had moved his heavy guns west of the canal and had been ready to drop back to the GHQ Line if things had got much worse. But the Germans claimed no great victory on that day. They were dismayed at the collapse of their attack caused by the intervention of just one 'fresh' brigade. It revealed that the German attack had relied once too often on a severely tested group of units, and that their objective was more in the nature of a diversion to cover the despatch of formations to the Eastern Front than a serious attempt to collapse the Salient further. They were content to have retained Hill 60. Their accounts are all of the 'great counter-attack' (in reality by just three exhausted battalions) 'that was only stopped at Frezenburg threw the Fourth Army on the defensive, and compelled the XXVI Reserve Corps and also the XXVII Reserve Corps to abandon the position captured. Only the XV Corps held its ground'. This report is actually more pessimistic than the real situation as the British did not reach Frezenburg, progressing no further than Verlorenhoek, and it simply shows what a shock the day was to the German High Command.

At Hill 60 survivors of the failed attack of the day before were making their way back to the British lines. A wounded Captain King of 2nd KOYLI told how he had got into the enemy lines with just eight men. He had seen them succumb to enemy fire one by one; he was the only survivor. One report spoke of Yorkshiremen still fighting on between the first and second German lines, subsisting on raw potatoes and muddy water, with no thought of surrender.

The Gas Attacks: Ypres 1915

9 May: A Really Satisfactory Infantry Fight

Next day the French began their great offensive in Artois, and the BEF attacked at Aubers Ridge in support of them. This would give the Germans something to think about while taking some of the pressure off the Ypres Salient: 1st British Cavalry Division was moved up in support of the battered 28th Division; 12th Brigade went into the line in and around Mouse Trap Farm.

The 9th of May saw the Germans keep up the pressure on 27th Division. From 5.30 am to 2 pm a heavy bombardment developed along the whole divisional front. One platoon of 2nd Gloucesters was killed to the last man, an unusual event even in modern warfare. The German infantry rushed the position and the Gloucesters immediately counter-attacked before they got too well established. In the fierce fighting the Gloucesters had their commander, Lieutenant Colonel Tulloch, and forty men killed and ninety more wounded to no avail, as the enemy could not be shifted.

That afternoon the shelling steadily escalated until 2 pm. There was a thirty-minute pause as if the German artillery was catching its breath. It was moving up more ammunition and coordinating the next phase of the fire programme. The shelling resumed at 2.30 pm and reached a crescendo at 4 pm with twenty minutes of stupendous fire of all calibres. Then the German infantry charged across about 250 yards of No Man's Land in three closely packed lines, suggesting they were relying on a large number of new drafts in their front-line units. The attack was destroyed by the British rifle and machine-gun fire of 3rd and 4th KRRC, 4th RB and 2nd KSLI. The Germans were seen to lose hundreds of men before running back. The whole process was repeated once more before the attacks stopped for the day. Brigadier General Croker personally inspected the front lines and advised against any further counter-attacks. The enemy had used fallen trees to make a very effective abattis covering their shell-hole positions.

This is how 2nd King's Shropshire Light Infantry recorded the day:

On the 9th about 6 am the enemy started shelling our line and continued until 2 pm, all firing then ceased for about half an hour, when it suddenly recommenced with increased intensity working systematically up and down the line. Soon after four o'clock the shelling developed into an absolute furnace of fire. For twenty minutes this rain of shells continued. Shells of every description, from 'Jack Johnsons' to 9-pounders, fell in and about our trenches. Suddenly it ceased. It was obvious that an infantry attack was coming, and an order to clean rifles was passed along.

Almost at once a line of Germans appeared over the crest of the hill some 250 yards in front. This line was followed by a second and then a third. On they came, shoulder to shoulder, their lines stretching right across the front. The troops hailed this apparition with deep satisfaction; here at last was something they could deal with. The enemy was met with a heavy and accurate fire. His lines melted away, some lay down, some turned and ran. Then it was seen that many of the enemy were wearing British uniform, and these came on shouting to our men. The battalion took no notice, but continued to fire. The Royal Fusiliers [on their left], however, ceased firing, though only for about twenty seconds, but it was twenty seconds of valuable time lost.

The enemy rallied and came on again over the ridge. He was again met by a heavy fire, which he could not face, but turning round fled in disorder. This brought to an end a really satisfactory infantry fight, which made up to the troops for a great deal of their sufferings under the appalling bombardment they had endured.

The battalion losses over four days, mostly incurred on 9 May, totalled 122; 4th KRRC were reduced to three officers and 100 men, having lost fifteen officers and 478 other ranks. Sir John French delivered a speech to 80th Brigade when it came out of the line a few days later. Denying Ypres to the Germans was influencing whole nations in their attitude to the war, he said, as he announced that Italy was declaring itself on the side of the Allies. The men would have appreciated hearing from Sir John:

To remain in the trenches under a heavy artillery bombardment, to keep your heads and your discipline, and to be able to use your rifles at the end of it, require far higher standards of personal bravery than actively to attack the enemy when everybody is on the move and conscious of doing something.

I see before me famous old regiments whose battle honours show that they have upheld the British Empire in all parts of the world in many famous battles, but I tell you that the battle you have just fought will rank higher than any that your regiments have to show on your colours.

The 2nd Royal Dublin Fusiliers thought this day in terms of German shelling was their worst experience in the war to date. The shelling, the accuracy of the enemy sniping and the closeness of the machine-gun fire made the mere act of holding their trenches, about 150 yards south-east of Mouse Trap Farm, an ordeal, and the idea of improving them 'a work of great difficulty'.

10 May

On 10 May the persistent shelling of 27th Division, rising in intensity between 10.30 am and 1.30 pm, went on all day. At about noon German infantry were seen massing for an attack. The British front-line trenches were very badly smashed about and large sections were quite buried. But the support line, some 300 yards back, was well constructed and concealed, with perfect fields of fire. The enemy infantry attack was soundly defeated. Later a small release of poison gas was tried against 2nd Cameron Highlanders and 1st Royal Scots, but the new British respirators worked very well and the attack was repulsed.

At 6 pm the German infantry came forward again but, as the defenders rose in their trenches to give fire, the attackers went to ground, digging in and refusing to close with the British. The Royal Engineers came forward to improve the support lines, but the German artillery had done such extensive damage to the forward positions that further work was seen to be pointless, and the whole line had to fall back to a prepared second line, from Bellewaarde Lake to Sanctuary Wood. As 4th Rifle Brigade withdrew they were closely pursued, and they were obliged to toss their machine guns into Bellewaarde Lake to prevent their capture. On reaching the line manned by the Argyll and Sutherland Highlanders, the Germans did not press home their attack; 4th Rifle Brigade had lost fifty killed, 300 wounded and forty-six men missing in the two-day battle. Two of their companies had no officers left at all.

Back at Ypres the shattered 83rd Brigade was temporarily organised as a composite battalion, commanded by Colonel Gough, 3rd Monmouths. His battalion formed one company of four officers and 130 men under Captain Gattie. Just three months ago the battalion had arrived in France with thirty-eight officers and 1,020 other ranks. Their Captain Steel had to command 2nd East Yorkshires as they had lost their entire complement of officers. For the Monmouths the battle was effectively over. They would observe the great fight of 24 May from reserve positions. Later that year all three battalions of Monmouths had to be amalgamated into one.

11 May

The 11th of May saw another day when, though they were generally in a defensive mode, the Germans made significant small gains by the relentless pressure kept up by their artillery and the ability of their infantry to exploit the opportunities thus created. Shelling south of the Menin Road went on from 7.30 to 11 am, and a gas cloud was released against 2nd Cameron Highlanders. The wind suddenly veered about and blew the gas back onto the two German infantry battalions delivering a close order attack. One British machine gun got onto the ensuing flight and did great execution.

Despite reinforcement, and a further attack being repulsed, the British trenches were collapsing under the weight of artillery fire and the Camerons and Argyll and Sutherlands were obliged to abandon the front trenches and fall back to the support line. The Germans followed up closely and seized the high ground (which the Germans called Hill 55) where the Menin Road bent slightly at the north-east corner of Sanctuary Wood. Three battalions (1st Royal Scots, 2nd Gloucesters and 1st Leinsters) scrapped for the position all night but at dawn it remained in German hands. B Company 1st Leinsters first went up to support the line, under the splendidly named Captain Wildblood. The Royal Scots and Camerons retook a lost trench late in the day but lost it again soon after. At 11 pm A and C Companies 1st Leinsters were ordered to deliver another counter-attack. It was dark, the wooded terrain made things more difficult, and there was little ammunition available for artillery support. The Leinsters decided to deliver a silent bayonet charge. The shock effect worked and the Germans were turned out of the trench. But one of their machine guns enfiladed the trench very effectively. Losses mounted; Major Conyers, the commanding officer, was mortally wounded and the Leinsters were forced to retire. The same two companies attacked again and seized the low ridge just in front of the trench and managed to hold it through the night. At daylight the German artillery shelled them off it. The Leinsters lost two officers and twenty-one men killed, three officers and 138 men wounded, and a further fifty-five missing, presumed killed. The Gloucesters tried three times to retake the trench, now choked with the dead and wounded of both sides, to no avail.

The continual drain on battalions in the line, even when not attacked by enemy infantry, is illustrated by the state of 83rd Brigade when relieved on the night of 10/11 May: 2nd East Yorkshires was their strongest unit at five officers and 283 other ranks. All the other units in the brigade had to be formed into one composite battalion until drafts arrived to rebuild them. Next day a draft of 406 men arrived for the East Yorks, and it transpired that 350 of them were volunteers from North Staffordshire Regiment who had switched cap badges for a chance to get over to the front line more quickly (by 24 May they would be back up to strength with fourteen officers and 837 other ranks).

On 10 May 50th Division had been alerted to be ready to move back into the Salient. On 11 May 151st Brigade moved into the GHQ Line to relieve the cavalry there and they provided copious drafts of men for digging work under the supervision of the Royal Engineers. This work, involving anything from 300 to 800 men per battalion, went on for several nights.

12 May

If 12 May was a relatively 'uneventful' day, it was because of the mutual exhaustion of the contending armies. Second Army could only count two shattered battalions as being 'in reserve' (4th KRRC and the PPCLI). The 150th Brigade (50th Division) was given to 27th Division as a badly needed reinforcement; 5th Durham Light Infantry immediately went up to the front-line trenches to relieve some of the weary Regulars. More heavy artillery was made available, principally 5-inch howitzers and 60-pounder guns. The 1st and 3rd Cavalry Divisions were dismounted and took over the trenches of 28th Division, which went back for a long-overdue rest. They went into Army reserve, into camps to the west and south of Poperinghe. With a severely reduced infantry strength of 200 officers and 8,000 men, 28th Division reckoned its casualties in the fighting in April and May at some 15,000. The 84th Brigade was reorganised as a composite battalion until it could receive enough drafts to rebuild its four weak battalions. Because of the general shortage of manpower, battalions supposedly 'at rest' were continually being turned out for fatigue duties – digging trenches, road-mending, dumping stores etc.

Meanwhile, the ammunition shortage was reaching crisis proportions. On this day Second Army had to report that its 4.5-inch howitzers – a mainstay of the infantry divisions in both attack and defence – had completely run out of shells of any description. The BEF was quick to point the finger of blame at the Gallipoli expedition, launched on 25 April 1915, at the height of the fighting in the Salient. Some 2,000 rounds of 4.5-inch and 20,000 rounds of 18-pounder shell desperately needed on the Western Front had been sent to the Dardanelles. It was a classic illustration of the real inability of Great Britain to sustain two major land campaigns in the spring of 1915, to the detriment of both. The resulting 'Shell Scandal' in the newspapers would lead to the creation of a Liberal-Conservative coalition government, and would cost the First Lord of the Admiralty, Winston Churchill, his job.

The shortages embraced more than just artillery ammunition. The BEF was below its established strength for machine guns (by forty-two) and its reserves of small-arms ammunition (0.303-inch bullets) were down to ninety-three rounds per rifle – enough for about ten minutes of close combat. Infantry drafts were arriving in France and Flanders without rifles, hoping to collect them on their way to the front from men who had no immediate need of them (supposedly something that only happened in the Russian Army in the First World War!). The recent fighting at Aubers Ridge had been a depressing failure, but the BEF was being steadily reinforced by the arrival of New Army divisions of 'Kitchener' volunteers: 9th (Scottish), 12th (Eastern) and 14th (Light)

Divisions were added to the order of battle, though the latter was delayed for the total want of ammunition.

Things were just as bad on the other side of the hill. The Royal Flying Corps reported large numbers of trains leaving Belgium, carrying men and material away to the east, where German armies were heavily engaged on the Russian front. No new formations arrived to help the German Fourth Army. A major attack at Ypres was planned for 13 May but it had to be postponed because of an acute shortage of artillery ammunition. The Germans were able to keep up a persistent shelling of the British lines but did not have the reserves for a major attack.

13 May

When the dismounted cavalry moved into the trenches of 28th Division, from Bellewaarde Lake to a point 600 yards south-east of Mouse Trap Farm, they found a line that had only been dug a few days before, and demonstrably without the assistance of the Royal Engineers. The trenches were 'poor, with little or no barbed wire in front and no communication trenches behind'. At 8 am 13 May, on a wet and muddy day, German infantry got into the trenches held by 7th Cavalry Brigade (Leicestershire Yeomanry, and 1st and 2nd Life Guards, with barely 300 men apiece). The troopers had no hand grenades at all with which to respond as the Germans began bombing their way along the trenches. A steady rifle fire from the Leicestershire Yeomanry in the support trench prevented the Germans from exploiting their success. Elsewhere 5th Dragoon Guards and 18th Hussars, together with the London Rifle Brigade (5th Londons) and 1st East Lancashires (of 4th Division) found themselves shelled out of their front-line trenches. These potential gaps in the line were covered by troops in the supports, and were recovered later in the day from each flank. One such gap was covered by a handful of the London Rifle Brigade, under Lance Sergeant Douglas Belcher, and their heavy and accurate rifle fire kept the Germans well at bay throughout the day. For his leadership Belcher became the first Territorial NCO to be awarded the Victoria Cross.

Since 8 May 1st Rifle Brigade had been responsible for the Mouse Trap Farm sector of the front. On 13 May they observed German bayonets assembling in a forward trench as the shelling increased markedly. Between 4 am and 4.50 am some trenches collapsed under the fire. The reserve company was positioned to cover the worst parts. At 7 am the centre and left of the battalion was attacked but the Germans were driven off. At about 7.30 am the retirement of the East Lancashires referred to above took place on the right of 1st RB. From the reserve lines 2nd Essex were sent forward, ostensibly to deliver a counter-attack but really to reinforce the front. They had to advance half a mile over open country, losing 180 men along the way; 1st Rifle Brigade stood and cheered them in as they reached the 'safety' of the front trenches. Meanwhile the RB machine guns, firing from the parados, drove off an attack on the right sub-sector. Two further small attacks were defeated but casualties mounted relentlessly, and the whole of the reserve company was drawn into the front trenches.

At some stage in the day the German artillery concentrated its fire on Mouse Trap Farm. One observer counted 100 shells a minute falling on the battered strongpoint. At dusk men of the East Lancashires pushed out towards the ominously silent position. They found that every single man of the two platoons of 1st Rifle Brigade there had been killed. The Hampshires to the left had seen the destruction wrought there and had extended their line to cover the gap caused. Though the enemy had sapped to within 30 yards of the farm it remained a bastion of the British front line.

It was a day of wearyingly persistent shellfire, and small-scale infantry attacks that were all beaten off. When the shelling died down later in the day the exasperated men of 11th Brigade stood up in their front line, jeering at the enemy and daring them to come on, which must have been something of a satisfying emotional release from the strains of the day.

The gap in the line held by 7th Cavalry Brigade could not be directly observed, but was covered by the Leicestershire Yeomanry in the support line. Still it posed a threat and 8th Cavalry Brigade (Royal Horse Guards, 10th Hussars and Essex Yeomanry) were moved up in the morning for a counter-attack. The artillery bombardment that should have started at noon failed to materialise. It began at 2 pm and at 2.30 the attack began, joined by the Leicestershire Yeomanry. Part of the line was regained temporarily but could not be held under the volume of fire developed by the Germans. A shell-hole line about 1,000 yards back, and well placed on a reverse slope, was

Some Trench Terminology

Ideally, trenches were laid out in systems to be mutually supporting – a front line, support line and reserve line. Each 'line' was itself a system of three trenches. The 'front line' comprised the fire trench (with a 'firestep' from which the men fought), a support trench and a reserve trench, with short connecting trenches between each line. These trench lines were interrupted along their length by earthen 'traverses', dividing the trench into 'fire bays', to prevent the whole line of the trench from being enfiladed. Some 400 to 600 yards further back would be the support line of three trenches, designed to hold those infantry needed to provide immediate assistance to the front line if attacked. Further back again was the reserve line, where some rest might be obtained and which housed headquarters and support units. All these three lines should be connected by communication trenches, to allow men and materials to move between them under cover.

The earth thrown forward when digging a trench formed a barricade called the 'parapet'. Earth thrown behind the trench formed the 'parados'. In Flanders the water table was so high that trenches could rarely be dug deeper than 3 feet. The trenches, so-called, were mostly barricades of sandbags built up to a height sufficient for protection from enemy fire.

Every morning at dawn, and every evening at dusk, there was a one-hour 'Stand To'. All men in the front line stood ready to resist any attempt the enemy might make in the half-light at that hour.

dug into a new line and occupied. For extra security, 151st Brigade (50th Division) was moved into the GHQ Line immediately behind it.

The cavalry, already weak in numbers compared to infantry units, had a bad day. A brigadier general was wounded in action; the Leicestershire Yeomanry had lost twelve officers and 175 men out of a total strength of 281. Both 27th and 4th Divisions on either side of them took over sections of their front-line trench to relieve some of the pressure they faced.

The German accounts of the day's fighting are pessimistic. They had clearly hoped for better things. Now Fourth Army was ordered to send some of its scarce artillery ammunition down to Sixth Army, fighting the Anglo-French offensives in the Artois region of France. Soon after it had to release 38th Landwehr Brigade and 202nd Reserve Infantry Regiment to Sixth Army. Far from receiving reinforcement, the tired infantrymen of Fourth Army were having to work even harder. The fact that there is no official German narrative for the whole period from 13 to 24 May suggests that they were glad of some rest. German strength and casualty returns – always a controversial subject – are incomplete for this battle. We know that 51st Reserve Infantry Division went from 343 officers and 12,993 men in April 1915, down to 224 officers and 8,712 men in May, with no clue as to how many replacements were drafted to make up their losses in the sustained fighting. Similarly, 52nd Reserve Infantry Division went from 343 officers and 13,551 men in April to 247 officers and 9,234 men in May.

14–23 May: An Interlude

The 14th of May saw just a few local flare-ups from the fighting of the previous day. At the notorious 'hot spot', Mouse Trap Farm, an attempt was made to attack from the German sap that had been driven to within 30 yards of the position. The British had two platoons in the farm area, now something of a crater field, two in close support and two more nearby, on hand if needed. The German infantry that broke into the position were quickly expelled and things went quiet there. Between Hooge and Bellewaarde a concentration of German infantry was spotted in good time, and broken up by British artillery.

There followed a distinct lull in activity, lasting nine days. Both sides spent it improving their front positions, their communication trenches and signals arrangements. The British greatly improved their anti-gas measures, with gas alarms well placed, and a steady improvement in personal protection. The first sixteen of the new gas helmets to reach each battalion were issued to the machine-gun crews. More heavy artillery became available to the BEF, and, when 28th Division returned to the front, the Cavalry Corps remained in place to give 27th Division its period of badly-needed rest and reorganisation.

The battered battalions absorbed the new drafts coming out from England, but invariably remained well below normal strength. Even after 150 reinforcements 4th KRRC had to be composited with the PPCLI for ten days before both were back to a fit state for further duty. The Rifles were surprised and pleased to receive one draft of forty-one very fit Fijians, who were promptly formed into a platoon and sent to B Company; 2nd Buffs were rebuilt with a draft of five officers and 350 other ranks.

The front lines at Ypres were never truly 'quiet' but there was, at least, a reduction in the level of violence experienced during the German assaults aimed at collapsing the Salient. Units that were in the line on the southern margins of the Salient usually found themselves left in place for as along as five weeks without relief: 1st Lincolns (9th Brigade, 3rd Division) was one such, guarding the flank between Hill 60 and the Comines Canal. They adopted a very aggressive stance, dominating No Man's Land by a series of nightly fighting patrols. Parties of NCOs and men worked all night of 15 May clearing vegetation from in front of their parapets without any interference from the enemy at all, which they took to be a sure sign of their moral ascendancy in that part of the line. Their thirty-five-day tour of duty would still cost them eight officers and 125 men as casualties to artillery and small-arms fire.

*

On 15 May the French 153rd Infantry Division launched an attack east of the canal, seizing some German-held houses at Steenstraat near the canal bridge there. This left the last German position west of the canal, a farm just south of Steenstraat, hopelessly vulnerable. Next day General Putz ordered 45th and 152nd French Infantry Divisions to join 153rd in finishing the job. The farm was stormed and, despite heavy counter-attacks delivered by the German XXII Reserve Corps, the French defenders held firm. That night the Germans evacuated their last foothold on the west bank of the canal. Their official account reported: 'The battles of the XXII Reserve Corps came to an end, as on the night of 16/17 May the west bank was abandoned. The losses of the troops, particularly in officers, had been very heavy.'

The 'Detachment d'Armée de Belgique' was reorganised as XXXVI Corps of the French Army. The four divisions, under General Hély d'Oissel, numbered about 33,000 infantry. The original two, 45th (Colonial) and 87th (Territorial), had been joined by 152nd and 153rd. There would always be French troops serving on the left flank of the British in the Salient, together with the steady Belgian Army. On 23 May Italy joined the Allied cause by declaring war on Austria. The war spread to yet another front, placing still further logistical strains on all participants. Meanwhile the Germans were winning great victories in Russia, and the campaign in Gallipoli had degenerated into the very trench warfare it had been designed to circumvent. A brief upsurge of unrestricted submarine warfare instituted by the Germans led to the loss of SS *Lusitania*, with a large number of Americans numbered amongst the civilian dead. CSM Shephard, 1st Dorsets, wondered, 'Is the blood of America composed of milk and water? . . . Surely no man can read of this Lusitania affair without the desire to avenge the poor dear little kiddies and helpless women who were lost.' He listed the increasing 'frightfulness' resorted to by the enemy – poison gas, the sinking of civilian shipping, the air raids on England – and surmised, 'All these things point to the enemy being in desperate straights [*sic*] and trying to win thro' by these methods, or in any case doing all the damage possible.' With a typical soldierly disdain for politicians he went on to opine, 'Meanwhile, we hear that our British Cabinet has held a meeting to consider whether or no we shall retaliate by using poisonous gases, resulting in the decision not to take action at present. Meanwhile, until they do decide to take retaliatory measures, the Cabinet should (in the opinion of a humble soldier) be placed on Hill 60. They would not hesitate long.'

Going into the last week of May 1915, V Corps was holding a 5½-mile front in the Salient. On the right was 83rd Brigade (28th Division); next, astride the Menin Road, came 1st Cavalry Division; then 85th Brigade (28th Division); 10th Brigade (4th Division) was in and around Mouse Trap Farm; 12th Brigade (4th Division) carried the line up to its junction with French XXXVI Corps. To strengthen some of the depleted units in these formations the whole infantry of 50th (Northumbrian) Division (TF) had been distributed amongst them – 149th Brigade to 4th Division, 150th Brigade to the Cavalry Corps, and 151st Brigade to 28th Division. Adequate reserves were in place – 84th Brigade (28th Division), 2nd Cavalry Division, 11th Brigade (4th Division), 13th Brigade (5th Division, but serving with 4th). In addition 27th Division and 3rd Cavalry Division were at rest near to hand.

24–25 May: Mutual Exhaustion

The first great supply of chlorine gas and cylinders used in the fighting so far had been utilised to the full. German industry had replenished the supply of both. There was to be one more great effort to use the gas weapon to reduce the Salient further.

The Biggest Gas Attack

After a period of heavy, stormy rain the British trenches were left knee-deep in mud and, in places, in danger of falling in. Monday 24 May 1915 was to be a fine, hot day. It was light as early as 2.30 am and, within a quarter of an hour, enemy signal flares were seen, heralding the start of a very heavy bombardment. Almost at once enemy machine-gun and rifle fire joined the attack, and the largest gas cloud yet seen was released on a 4^1/$_2$-mile front from just south of Hooge to just short of Turco Farm, where the French lines began. Its effects were reported up to 5 miles away. At one point the trenches were so close together that British infantry reported hearing the hiss of the gas as it left the cylinders. Carried by a light but steady east wind, the cloud rose to 40 feet in height and moved inexorably over No Man's Land and the front trenches. It was so thick that it reportedly obscured houses as it passed by. It would still be strong when it reached the canal at about 6 am, and it was discernible up to 20 miles behind the front line. One Dublin Fusilier left this graphic description as the German gas came 'drifting down wind in a solid bank some 3 miles in length and 40 feet in depth, bleaching the grass, blighting the trees, and leaving a broad scar of destruction behind it'. The worst of the gas hit 10th and 12th Brigades of 4th Division.

Inevitably, especially where the trenches were closest together, some men fumbled with their respirators and fell victim to the gas. But in the main the British were alert and ready to receive such an attack. British officers were now well used to assessing the wind conditions each day, and expected an attack whenever a firm easterly wind blew. What they could not predict was the sheer violence of this particular assault. Four German divisions, supported by a powerful artillery, crashed into four British brigades – 39th Infantry Division (XV Corps) attacked at Hooge; 53rd and 54th Reserve Infantry Divisions (XXVII Reserve Corps) from Bellewaarde to Wieltje, and 51st Reserve Infantry Division (XXVI Reserve Corps) north-west of Ypres. The bombardment, heavily laced with tear gas shells, went on at a high tempo for four and a half hours. A particular problem for the defenders was the rapid loss of all telephone links with the front line, which was covered in dense smoke and dust, making it extremely difficult for commanders to assess the course of the battle and make the necessary adjustments. Attempts to repair the vital cables were in vain. Each battalion in the front line was reduced to defending its own sector and hoping that its neighbours were holding their own.

The Loss of Mouse Trap Farm

Still the first rush by German infantry was beaten off all along the line, except at one point. The two platoons of Royal Dublin Fusiliers manning Mouse Trap Farm were overwhelmed by attackers emerging through the gas cloud from the enemy trenches just 30 yards away. This extraordinary, long-lived strongpoint fell at last. A report by Captain Leahy, the only line officer on his feet at the end of the day, recounts the last moments at the Farm: the 'scruffy', admirable Colonel Loveband, his second-in-command, Major Magan, the battalion's medical officer, Doctor Russell, and the Adjutant, Captain Leahy had just finished dinner in their dug-out at 2.30 am. Loveband had been round all the trenches, especially Mouse Trap Farm, and had warned them that the weather conditions made it a likely night for gas, and checked the sprayers, respirators and gas alarms. At 2.45 am Loveband and Leahy were just outside their dug-out when they saw red flares over various parts of the German trenches. Then a dull roar began and they saw the gas cloud coming either side of Mouse Trap Farm. Loveband called out: 'Get your respirators, boys, here comes the gas!' That was only just in time; Doctor Russell was helping others into their masks and was late getting into his own.

The routine morning 'Stand To' was just over and the daily rum ration was being issued, so everyone was awake and alert. The breeze was gentle and it took the gas three-quarters of an hour to pass over the RDF lines; it crossed over the trenches but lingered longer about battalion headquarters. Company A was not badly affected, but 9th Argyll and Sutherland Highlanders next door got hit badly. Loveband and Leahy had to run out and stop a group of the Highlanders moving to the rear without orders. They caught five Dublins in that group and returned three of them to duty as orderlies; the other two were badly gassed.

Loveband and Leahy could see men leaving the trenches to the left of the farm and Germans were observed closing in on the right-hand corner. At 4.45 am Loveband fired off three messages: to the nearest men of 9th A&SH to counter-attack at once; to the King's Own and 18th Royal Irish warning them that the Germans had got into the front line; to the commander of 9th A&SH asking him to send two companies up for a counter-attack. The telephone wires to brigade headquarters were cut. The King's Own replied they were in control of their section, and would be able to assist 18th Royal Irish.

As the gas gradually cleared heavy shelling intensified. Men of the Argyll and Sutherland Highlanders, including a machine-gun detachment, came up to the support lines but could not get further forward towards Mouse Trap Farm. At 5.55 am Loveband again requested two companies of A&SH to counter-attack towards the farm. He had to use runners for this message as all wires were cut. Every one of the runners was hit and he had to resort to using gassed men and battalion signallers as runners to get the message through.

Loveband finally got a message through to 10th Brigade, that the Germans were in Mouse Trap Farm and 'things were not looking good'. He needed reinforcements to counter-attack the enemy. German artillery was now sending over lachrymatory gas shells. Major Magan was gassed out of action; Doctor Russell was badly wounded but worked on. Colonel Poole (Warwicks) came up to assess the situation. Soon after he left, Loveband, Leahy and the signals officer were standing behind their headquarters when bullets were fired from behind and the Colonel was hit in the heart and died trying to say something. The signals officer was also hit and rushed off to try to get the shooting to stop. This suggests one of those tragic 'friendly fire' incidents, where British troops coming up from the support lines had inadvertently fired on the command group of 2nd RDF.

By now British heavy artillery was plastering the farm area, as were the Germans. German infantry had completely overrun the 18th Royal Irish trenches on the right and had quickly consolidated them for their own use. The Highlanders were drawn away to the right to meet this threat, men began falling back in disorder. Captain Leahy and the tireless Doctor Russell ran out and brought some Dublins back into line but most of the men retiring were hit. The defenders were down to one man for every 5 yards of front. The line stabilised along the support trenches. More and more men in the front trenches were surrounded and losses mounted relentlessly. The last message, sent at 12.45 read: 'Reinforce or all is lost.'

From about 2.30 pm no fighting could be heard in the front trenches of the Royal Dublin Fusiliers; everyone there had held onto them to the last; there was no surrender, no quarter given or accepted; they all died fighting at their posts. The trench strength of the battalion in the morning had been seventeen officers and 651 other ranks. Answering the evening roll call that day were just one wounded officer and twenty men. Twelve officers had been killed; four wounded; one was missing. Even after receiving a draft of reinforcements the battalion only reached four officers (including the chaplain and the medical officer) and 190 other ranks. There was no shame attached to the final loss of Mouse Trap Farm.

Reluctant Attackers?

On the front of 85th Brigade two companies of 8th Middlesex and one company of 2nd East Surreys were hit so severely as to be described as 'annihilated'. 8th Middlesex would lose eleven officers out of fourteen and 200 men out of 374 during the day. But the rest of 2nd East Surreys, together with 9th Durham Light infantry, and a later reinforcement from 8th DLI, held their positions throughout the day.

An officer of 2nd East Surreys wrote home with an intriguing description of the German attack, suggesting that the German infantry was rapidly losing interest in these costly proceedings:

> In the attack last Monday the Germans attacked on a front of several miles and must have been there in thousands, as there seemed to be no end of them. After a furious bombardment lasting several hours, and after gassing us, the infantry advanced: in front of us they massed in some woods, and then they emerged – it was a wonderful sight; they walked across the fields in our direction without any order, sometimes two or three men together, sometimes five or six or more; there was no attack as we understand it; they simply looked like a crowd coming away from a race meeting, just a mob.
>
> They did not double; they never stopped to fire; they simply moved stolidly forward regardless of losses; they were twice held up and retired, but receiving a fresh impetus from the rear, they came on again; they got to about 200 yards from us and, unable to advance any further, dug themselves in; they are extraordinarily good at this as they disappear into the earth in a very short time. Of course, the infantry advance is covered by an overwhelming fire from their artillery and machine-guns, so that our infantry do not have altogether a pleasant time, and it is rather wonderful that they inflict the losses they do.

The East Surreys would record losses of eleven killed, thirty-four wounded and seventy-five missing in action for the day. Two officers and twenty-four men were gassed, of whom two soldiers later died.

Once the Germans had made a small penetration of the front line, between 8th Middlesex and 2nd East Surreys, they began to bomb along the trench, rolling up 3rd Royal Fusiliers and 7th DLI. Three companies of 2nd Buffs were sent up from brigade reserve but were under such heavy fire that few of the men made it into position. The survivors rallied behind Railway Wood and did well to maintain their position there for the rest of the day. The 8th Durham Light Infantry also advanced very steadily across open ground, and under a heavy fire, to add their strength to the defenders. Major Johnson, commanding 3rd Royal Fusiliers, was ordered to counter-attack and restore the line, and was told two companies of the Buffs would assist. But in the confusion of battle, only one company and a handful of other Fusiliers, and two platoons of Buffs, could be got together to advance on an enemy-occupied ridge some 200 yards off. Johnson was wounded in the hopeless attack and his men were forced to go to ground. The Germans worked their way in behind them, despite the help from the Buffs. The Royal Fusiliers had shrunk in strength from 880 to about 150 in the firing line (inevitably there were numbers of men mixed up with other units). With the Buffs, they did well to hold on to the third-line trenches until the end of the day. They had only one officer left out of eighteen, and their confirmed loss of 536 other ranks is reckoned to be the worst single day's casualty list for any of the many battalions of Royal Fusiliers in the Great War. Brigadier General Pereira, the new GOC 85th Brigade, considered launching another counter-attack with two weak companies of 3rd Middlesex and a handful of Buffs. Major General Bulfin pointed out that it would take two full brigades to do the job, and 85th Brigade was told to stay firmly on the defensive.

Near Hooge the gas cloud had fortuitously missed most of 1st Cavalry Brigade's front, and they were able to beat off the attackers with ease. But, just as unluckily, the gas hit 2nd Cavalry Brigade very badly just north of the Menin Road, between Hooge and Bellewaarde. In a desperate effort to prevent a break in, the whole of the divisional reserve, 9th Cavalry Brigade, was drawn into the fighting. The line held – just. Brigadier General Mullen and his Brigade Major were gassed. Then, at about 10 am, the German 39th Division launched a renewed assault and broke the line of 18th Hussars, just as 3rd Royal Fusiliers were bombed out of their trenches on the left: 18th Hussars, whose ranks were 50 per cent new drafts under fire for the first time, ended the day with just six officers left out of fifteen, and fifty-seven men out of 273. As German infantry flowed through the small gap the nearest units in the area, 9th Lancers and 4th Green Howards, lined a communication trench and brought them to a halt. Other local troops were scraped together, including 150 men of A Company 2nd Buffs, and, as a composite force of a few hundred, they were able to plug the gap and prevent any further exploitation by the enemy. The single company of the Buffs found itself manning 500 yards of fire trench, and also had to throw back a flank guard as they could see Germans who had gone as far as 1,000 yards past their open left flank. Joined by 5th Durham Light Infantry, they were able, from their assembly point in Zouave Wood, to threaten the flank of any Germans that pushed through the gap. The 9th Lancers were grateful for the assistance and admitted that, when the infantry arrived, their men were 'on their knees'. A poignant story is recorded by 5th DLI. One of their platoons was assailed by a party of Germans that had worked its way through the woods and got behind them. In the firefight a German officer and sergeant leading the attack were killed. Soon after a young German was seen crawling up behind a hedge, calling out in German 'Father, father!' He was shot and wounded but made his escape. A later search of the dead sergeant's pockets revealed a photograph of the sergeant and the young soldier standing together.

Good Gas Discipline

On the left 4th Division had 10th and 12th Brigades in the front line. The Royal Irish Fusiliers had particularly good gas discipline and hardly lost a man as the gas cloud passed over them. They beat off the heavy attack coming in behind it. They had 5th Border Regiment attached for training purposes. Everyone remarked how these men, many of them coal miners, were not much bothered by the gas and fought on manfully beside the steady Regulars. However, 2nd Royal Dublin Fusiliers (who had been forcefully put out of Mouse Trap Farm) and 7th Argyll and Sutherland Highlanders found themselves under terrible pressure. The weak 9th Argylls, in the support trench about 100 yards behind, were ordered forward to stiffen the front. They ran up through the gas cloud and just managed to stabilise the line as it had started to crumble. Then 149th Brigade (50th Division) was moved into place as a reserve for this sector; most of the front-line battalions in 4th Division had a company of

'Northumbrian' infantry attached. While they rarely figure in accounts of these desperate battles, those battalions of the Northumberland Fusiliers engaged, and 5th Border Regiment, lost between 200 and 300 men each. Similarly, 1/4th East Yorkshires were distributed amongst the cavalry holding the Zouave Wood–Sanctuary Wood area, one company to each of three regiments, with one in reserve until it was drawn into the fighting in support of 4th Green Howards, 9th Lancers and 5th DLI. The battalion actually passed under the command of 2nd Cavalry Division that evening.

The 2nd Royal Irish (12th Brigade) manned the line near Irish Farm where it angled back towards the west. This meant that the gas cloud not only passed over half their front, but actually travelled down the length of the trench over the other half. They were badly affected by the gas, just as the Germans came bombing along the trenches from Mouse Trap Farm. Small reinforcements from 2nd Lancashire Fusiliers helped them to just hold on and no more. The Lancashire Fusiliers, and Royal Warwicks (of 10th Brigade) tried to coordinate a counter-attack, but the Germans had got their machine guns forward to the captured sections of the British front line. The counter-attack was broken up before it really got started. The local commanders realised that further such efforts were futile in the short term, and concentrated on defending the line.

The Germans were relentlessly and methodically clearing out the old British front line. Around noon 2nd Royal Dublin Fusiliers could not take any more. Ten of their officers were killed (including Lieutenant Colonel Loveband) and all the others were wounded: 'Organized defence came to an end.' The front collapsed rapidly. Of 2nd Royal Irish that evening only Regimental Sergeant Major Plunkett was left unwounded to rally the battalion and bring them out of the line. When the two reserve platoons rejoined, Lieutenant McKay found himself in command of the battalion as they bivouacked on the eastern bank of the canal. Lieutenant Colonel Moriarty and nine other officers had been killed, another three were in hospital gassed, and 379 men were lost. One company of the Lancashire Fusiliers was down to an officer and eight men.

Only the steady resistance of 9th Argyll and Sutherland Highlanders in the support trench kept the enemy at bay. The next defensible line was 1,000 yards to the rear, running from Wieltje Farm, via Hill Top Farm to Turco Farm, where the switch line rejoined the old front line. Excellent assistance was rendered by the French 75mm guns west of the canal. Their stream of accurate and heavy fire was directed over a good telephone link by an officer in 12th Brigade who spoke perfect French. In the old front line on the left 1st King's Own and 2nd Essex delivered a devastating volume of accurate rifle fire that kept the enemy well away. As the day progressed it was clearly felt that the enemy pressure was diminishing.

Another Futile Counter-Attack

Having been directed that a strong counter-attack was required to restore the situation, 28th Division called up 84th and 80th Brigades for the purpose: 84th Brigade had been on a high state of alert since 5.15 am, when 2nd Cheshires had been ordered forward to the GHQ Line. There followed a sorry tale of rushed and uncoordinated arrangements that fell a long way short of expectations. 84th Brigade was a weak formation where only 1st Welch, at 600 men, had any real fighting strength. The 2nd Northumberland Fusiliers had been built back up to fifteen officers and 608 men, but not all of them were available for front-line duty. Their commanding officer was Captain Wreford Brown, though it was widely known he was not really medically fit to take a battalion into the front line. All the battalions were just about to eat a hot midday meal when they were ordered forward immediately. As the Northumberland Fusiliers passed a large draft of new troops just arriving, they were recognised by the draft's commander, Captain Salier, NF. He promptly handed the new soldiers over to a senior NCO and rejoined his battalion as Adjutant, a welcome relief to Wreford Brown. They went in south of Ypres, past the notorious and well-named Hellfire Corner, to the GHQ Line, under German artillery fire and taking losses, only to find 80th Brigade would not be there for some hours yet. They could have been left to have their hot meal in comfort and safety after all. At 2.30 pm the brigade was ordered to attack without waiting for 80th Brigade to arrive. Between delays caused by negotiating a way through the wire of the GHQ Line, lingering gas and the German shelling, it would be nearly 5 pm before the full attack could be organised, supported by the divisional artillery of 27th and 28th Divisions.

Instead 84th Brigade went ahead and attacked at 2.45 pm, with 2nd Northumberland Fusiliers (commanded by a captain) towards Wittepoort Farm, 2nd Cheshires (also commanded by a captain) on their left towards Railway Wood and 1st Suffolks (commanded by a major) dealing with the enemy just south of the Bellewaarde Lake. In support were 1st Welch; 1st Monmouths in reserve.

The 2nd Northumberland Fusiliers attacked in three company waves, keeping the fourth in reserve. They began their advance south of the Menin Road and, after about 300 yards, crossed it to the north. The Official History bases its description of the battle on the War Diary of 84th Brigade, but the brigade admits to a 'total ignorance' of what really occurred before about 7 pm. It fell to the compilers of battalion and regimental histories to gather in eyewitness accounts and record the battle for posterity. The attackers were not certain if Wittepoort Farm was occupied by the enemy, but a heavy machine-gun fire from there soon clarified the situation. It was serving as an outpost to the main German line and it disrupted the attack very effectively. It was late in the afternoon before the attackers got close enough to drive the defenders from the farm, by which time the battalion was severely weakened. As the attack petered out around dusk, Captain Wreford Brown was killed. Captain Salier took command, with only three officers and 'a handful of men' still on their feet.

With less than 400 men under arms, the Suffolks reached a point near Wittepoort Farm on the Menin Road at about 5 pm. Deploying two companies forward, with two in support, they crossed the road and lined a ditch, sheltered by a hedge. The Germans were about 100 yards off, on the edge of a wood. On the order to charge, the men rose up and pushed their way through the hedge. The whole first rank was shot down and the survivors fell back into the ditch. After making some small gains north of the Menin Road the brigade went to ground and dug in, expecting 80th Brigade to join them in a renewed effort. However, 80th Brigade (27th Division), though on the move forward since 6.30 am, had not been formally handed over to 28th Division until 1 pm. They didn't reach the GHQ Line until

7 pm, by which time the 84th Brigade attack had broken down. Time was lost trying to find the relevant headquarters to report to. It was 11 pm before two battalions, 4th Rifle Brigade and 3rd King's Royal Rifle Corps, joined the renewed attack by 84th Brigade, in what the KRRC called 'a haphazard affair' marked by 'maximum confusion'. Despite the bright moonlight, the attackers got within a few yards of the enemy trenches without severe loss. But then a storm of fire broke out, forcing them to fall back to their start line. They managed to hold on there, though exhausted and without any chance of food or water making it forward through the German barrage. Near midnight 1st Suffolks had renewed their attack, going in west of Wittepoort Farm on a 400-yard frontage. Once again a withering fire saw the men fall in heaps. When they returned to Ypres that night, only three officers and 181 men were on their feet. It had been an expensive effort.

A pitifully weak 2nd Northumberland Fusiliers were led forward yet again, by Captain Salier. In this last, hopeless effort, he was wounded, and one of his two subalterns was killed. At dawn on 25 May just one officer and six men were pinned down in shell holes immediately before the enemy trenches. They dashed back to safety and, in the rush, Second Lieutenant Freeman was twice wounded.

The incredible 2nd Northumberland Fusiliers lost another thirteen officers and 350 men; 2nd Cheshires ten officers and 279 men; 1st Suffolks had Major Maycock killed, losing nine other officers and 135 men; 1st Welch lost fifteen officers (including Colonel Marden wounded) and 418 men. 84th Brigade took 60 per cent casualties; of the battalion commanders, one was killed and three were wounded. The two battalions of 80th Brigade involved lost a further sixteen officers and 490 men.

Two companies of 2nd KSLI delivered an attack through Railway Wood that captured the German first line, but were defeated by the firm defence of the second line. At dawn the position was enfiladed from both flanks and was quite untenable. The British fell back to the Ypres–Menin Road and dug in. They then witnessed an extraordinary incident as a motor car raced up the road from Ypres, stopped between the British and German lines, picked up the abandoned kit of some cavalry officers, and flew back down again. The attack had cost them eight officers and 192 men. An officer of the neighbouring 1st Welch Regiment wrote to say how well the KSLI had performed in their attack. They had taken the pressure off the Welch, who were themselves forced to retire because they were under persistent and accurate shrapnel fire from their own artillery.

On the left the idea of counter-attacking to regain Mouse Trap Farm received a boost when it was reported that three French battalions would be made available to join the attack. When that effort was clarified to offering them in a support role only, the presence of Lieutenant Colonel A. A. Montgomery from the divisional staff, saw the counter-attack orders cancelled. Furthermore, this excellent staff officer – a future Chief of the Imperial General Staff – took a good look at the collapsed British front line, seeing how it bent back in a dangerous angle, and ordered 4th Division to fall back to much stronger defences 1,000 yards to the rear. The commander of 4th Division entirely approved of his decision. There the line was firmly anchored both to right and left and the whole position was much the better for it. The wounded were all got away safely and the withdrawal carried out without any further casualties.

The fighting was dying down all along the line. At dusk a company of 1st York and Lancasters emerged from Zouave Wood to drive some troublesome Germans out of houses along the Menin Road. They watched as the German garrison fled down the road, only to be fired on by their own people in the gloom and general confusion.

The Germans were deeply unhappy at the lack of overall success of this major attack. They awarded no battle honours to cover any of the fighting. The reports congratulated 51st Reserve Infantry Division for finally taking Wieltje Chateau (their name for Mouse Trap Farm) but concluded, 'This done, the troops were at the end of their power'. Indeed the German Fourth Army was so completely played out that the day ended with a formal order putting a stop to all further attacks in the Ypres Salient.

The Second Battle of Ypres was over.

Enough is Enough

The Allies, of course, did not know that at the time and waited anxiously on 25 May to see what the day held for them. There was persistent shelling throughout the day but no more infantry attacks. Ammunition supplies were critically low for both the British and German armies engaged. Liddell Hart suggests that it was the draining of German shell reserves that determined the end of the battle. 'For the Germans had at least the good sense to cease attacks when they came to the choice between economising infantry lives and economising artillery ammunition.' Both sides needed to rebuild the shattered formations that had sustained the fight since 22 April.

An address by Sir John French to his troops in May 1915, after thirty-three days of battle, must have helped some of them make sense of the dreadful ordeal:

> You held on to your trenches in the most magnificent manner under a more severe bombardment than has ever been known, and in doing so you have been of the greatest assistance to operations which the British Army was carrying out at the time. Men who have merely to lie down under a fire like that are apt to think that they are undergoing war rather than making war . . . By holding on to your trenches you prevented the Germans from obtaining an objective which it was very necessary for them to obtain. They wanted to take Ypres, and to be able to tell the whole of Europe and America that they had taken Ypres, and if they had done so this would have done us a lot of harm. This might have had the effect of keeping neutral nations out of the war. I can tell you that to-day Italy will declare war on behalf of the Allies. To remain in the trenches under a heavy artillery bombardment, to keep your heads and your discipline and to be able to use your rifles at the end of it, requires far higher qualities of personal bravery than actively to attack the enemy when everybody is on the move and conscious of doing something.

All or part of this address is reproduced in many of the unit histories covering this period of the war and suggests that the 'little Field Marshal' had a better understanding of military psychology than he is credited with. His words were chosen with care and feeling for the sensibilities of the old Regulars of the British Army and of the new troops coming out to the Western Front already deeply imbued with the love of regiment that is at the core of those sentiments.

30–31 July: The Flamethrower Attack at Hooge

Hooge was always a terrible part of the line. After the Second Battle of Ypres died away, the front line ran around the edge of Sanctuary Wood and across a shallow valley up to the Menin Road. Just across the road at Hooge it bent back at 90 degrees and ran parallel with the road past Hooge Chateau before bending outwards again and running north in front of Railway Wood. This sharp salient-within-a-salient, occupying a small prominence of value as an observation post, was an exceptionally dangerous scene of mining, shelling and probing attacks. The British defence was organised around the largest of several craters and the wretched trenches around it and leading up to it.

The British had been evicted from Hooge Chateau on 2 June. On 16 June they launched a series of attacks to recover the ground in what was now called the Bellewaarde Salient; 7th Brigade reported the gain of 250 yards on an 800-yard front, and the capture of over 200 prisoners and three machine guns. But as the fighting sucked in more and more battalions, and a mid-afternoon counter-attack proved almost suicidal, British losses soared. The 3rd Division finally reported losses of between 3,500 and 4,000 to the troops packed into an area some 1,000 yards square, subjected to intense German bombardment. The Germans then turned a captured British redoubt into a most formidable defensive position and the Tunnelling Companies of the Royal Engineers decided they would get them out of it. Working in saturated earth, where the mine gallery was always 6 inches deep in water, they drove a tunnel in under the German position and placed 3,500 pounds of ammonal high explosive. It was exploded at 7 pm on 19 July. In the resulting crater there was a pronounced lip some 15 feet above ground level, which is what made the craters so 'valuable' in this endless battle to secure any height advantage. The crater was rushed by 4th Middlesex and held after some desperate fighting with hand grenades, of which, according to every British account of such combat, the Germans seemed to have an inexhaustible supply.

In response to that attack the Germans were once more to demonstrate their intensely practical, value-free approach to war. Any weapon or action that might shorten the duration of organised violence as an instrument of state policy was to be embraced.

The 14th (Light) Division held the line around Hooge and noticed that one set of trench reliefs was not interfered with; the line had gone unnaturally quiet which was always a bad sign. 'The silence after we got into the line became uncanny.' The ensuing attack was so perfectly timed so soon after the relief that it was widely believed that German radio intercepts had discovered the upcoming changeover and laid their plans accordingly. The 'Stand To' at dawn on 30 July was suddenly interrupted by a German mine exploding under the chateau stables, and by a ferocious bombardment by artillery, trench mortars and machine guns, directed especially against the communication trenches and support lines out towards Zouave and Sanctuary Woods. But most memorably the British were attacked for the first time by liquid fire.

The Flammenwerfers

Apparently this weapon had been used once or twice against the French as early as October 1914 but had gone largely unnoticed. A device for projecting burning material had been seen in the fifth century BC, but it was in the early 1900s that the engineer, Richard Fiedler, and the Landwehr Pioneer officer, Reddemann, developed two types for the German Army. The *Klein-flammenwerfer* was carried by a single man on a backpack. Using a mix of pressurised air and carbon dioxide or nitrogen, it projected burning petroleum over a distance of 18 metres. The *Grossflammenwerfer* was not man-portable, and fired flame for forty seconds over nearly 40 metres. In 1911 three battalions of specialist troops were trained to use them.

On this day the flame attack was delivered at 3.22 am by nine large and eleven small projectors of *Flammenwerfer* Company Beck. The fixed *Grossflammenwerfer* fired first, each projecting obliquely across No Man's Land, building up a wall of flame that screened the advance of the portable *Kleinflammenwerfer* that fired straight into the British front line. We know that these troops did not suffer one fatal casualty in their subsequent triumph. The main assault was by the soldiers of 126th (Württemberg) Infantry Regiment, of 39th (Alsatian) Infantry Division, who left a record of the ferocity of the fighting and their admiration for the British resistance. They took only nineteen prisoners and 'had to storm all four machine guns directly to stop them'. The attack struck most severely against 8th Rifle Brigade, who had only relieved 7th RB at 2 am and had barely settled into the line. It came as a terrible shock; all eyewitnesses speak of the horror of the liquid fire. Second Lieutenant Carey recalled:

> There was a sudden hissing sound, and a bright crimson glare over the crater turned the whole scene red. As I looked I saw three or four distinct sheets of flame – like a line of powerful fire-hoses spraying fire instead of water – shoot across my fire trench. How long this lasted it is impossible to say – probably not more than a minute; but the effect was so stupefying that, for my own part, I was utterly unable for some moments to think collectedly.

Second Lieutenant Keith Rae was in the front line to the right of the crater and just in front of the stables with his platoon of C Company. He was last seen, terribly burned and wounded, standing on the parapet firing his revolver at the attackers. His body was lost and he is commemorated on the Menin Gate at Ypres. (His family put up a private memorial to him in the grounds of Hooge Chateau. New owners asked for it to be moved in 1968 and it now stands at Sanctuary Wood Cemetery.) Second Lieutenant Woodroffe kept his men holding a post until all their bombs were gone; then he extricated his command in good order. He was killed in the subsequent counter-attacks and was awarded a posthumous Victoria Cross, the first awarded to any of Kitchener's 'New Army'. The 8th Rifle Brigade lost nineteen out of twenty-four officers, and 469 out of 764 men.

The Germans seized the front line very quickly, with minimal losses, and then bombed along the trenches and got behind 7th KRRC. Assailed from all sides, they were thrust out of the line, losing nine officers killed, four wounded and 289 other ranks. Only 1/8th Sherwood Foresters, not attacked by liquid fire, hung on to their positions on the edge of Sanctuary Wood and did not let the Germans pass.

The Gas Attacks: Ypres 1915

A Counter-Attack Under Protest

At 2.45 pm the inevitable quick counter-attack was ordered by the corps commander, Sir John Keir: 7th RB and 8th KRRC, only just relieved, were ordered back in immediately, along with 9th KRRC. The local brigadier general commanding 41st Brigade (Oliver Nugent, later the commander of Ulster's 36th Division) protested about the lack of preparation. His message to divisional headquarters read: 'In my opinion situation precludes counter-attack by day. Counter-attack would be into a re-entrant and would not succeed in face of enfilade fire.' He thought it would take a full division and twelve hours of artillery bombardment to retake the lost trenches and craters. He was overruled. In particular it was thought 9th KRRC were well rested and fit and so they were selected to lead the attack. They were caught in enfilade fire and took heavy losses, including their commanding officer. Some ground was recovered but the attacks, delivered largely by men who had gone through the nightmare fighting of that morning, and moving up over clear fields of fire swept by machine guns, were bloodily defeated in the main. The 8th KRRC lost three officers killed, seven wounded, and 190 other ranks; 9th KRRC lost eight officers killed (including Lieutenant Colonel Chaplin), five wounded, and 333 other ranks. At the earliest opportunity, by 3.30 pm, Nugent, on his own authority, called the whole pointless exercise off. By then his fine brigade had barely 720 men fit to command. His ill-concealed bitterness in a letter to Lieutenant General Sir Edward Hutton, Colonel Commandant of the KRRC, is understandable:

> I cannot forget and I shall never forget or forgive the order that sent my brigade into the inferno of a counter-attack against an impossible position without Artillery preparation, in broad daylight, and after two days of strenuous work without food or water. The Brigade did all it could, no troops could have done better, but it was an impossible task and I went up and stopped any further attacks when I saw that the lines of men were simply being mown down in swathes as they came out of the woods . . . The curse of the Salient has been heavy on 14th Division.

The 6th Duke of Cornwall's Light Infantry had been called forward from Ypres as early as 5.26 am. They were caught by enemy shelling and lost Major J. Jones-Parry killed and thirty other ranks on the way up. A and B Companies moved up to Sanctuary Wood, and C and D Companies to Zouave Wood. They were able to send help to 8th Rifle Brigade as it struggled to stabilise the line they had been forced back upon. A captain wrote a description of the advance:

> We were ordered to follow the RB and attack, so we dashed over the open into Zouave Wood, D Company leading, followed by C Company. A and B were in Sanctuary Wood on our right. Paddison, commanding D, led them in a magnificent manner and the men of D were glorious, all shouting 'Let's avenge the poor old Major.' Paddison was killed by a shrapnel wound in the head. C Company followed and finally the 7th RB were held up by machine-gun fire at the far fringe of Zouave Wood . . . our men went on – and on . . . They lined Zouave Wood and held it. They were grand and nothing could move them.

In particular the bombers of the DCLI went up to assist in the preparing of hand grenades for use, by inserting the detonators into some 300 or 400 grenades in their boxes. Later another group of bombers were ordered forward over shell-swept ground to support the right flank of the RB. Sergeant Major Fred Keeling described his feelings in a letter home:

> I passed several men dead or horribly wounded; less wounded men were wending their way back to the dressing station. I felt cheerful nevertheless, really a sort of tinge of joy of battle in spite of the hellishness of it all, though you can't get a real joy of battle in these artillery days.

The 1/7th Sherwood Foresters (The Robin Hoods) secured the line in Sanctuary Wood. They originally dug in along the edge of the wood but were allowed to fall back some 70 yards, under better cover. It would remain a very dangerous place.

Having been subjected to heavy and accurate fire from German infantry on higher ground overlooking their trenches, the DCLI found themselves under attack at 2 am by bombers coming along two old communication trenches, covered by artillery fire. Suddenly the portable flamethrowers came into action again and the liquid fire sent the Cornwalls reeling back. Four regimental officers and the medical officer were killed in the chaos, and another eighty other ranks lost. Where some leaderless men broke and ran from the front line the machine-gunners behind them were so outraged at this 'stain' on the regiment's honour that they threatened to open fire on the retiring men if they did not go back. The Cornwall's were going 'to bloody well stick it' and the line was duly restored. They held on under fire from three sides without any food or water for forty-eight hours. When relieved by 6th KOYLI 6th Cornwalls had lost seven officers and 285 other ranks (thirty killed, fifty-five missing presumed killed and 200 wounded).

The 'Robin Hoods' spent the day improving their line and going out to rescue British soldiers wounded in the counter-attack of the day before. Their aggressive patrolling did much to clarify the situation and gathered important information that would be useful in the next great action fought at this hellish place.

The 41st Brigade had lost fifty-five officers and 1,181 other ranks, largely because of the wasteful counter-attack on the after-noon of 30 July.

9 August: Lessons Learned and Applied

The British were learning from their experiences all the time, and now a more organised counter-attack was planned. Leaving the crater area in German hands put an enormous strain on this sharp angle in the line and it was determined that the ground had to be retaken.

Congreve's 6th Division came into the line and gave a good demonstration of careful planning and first-class inter-arms cooperation. Plenty of guns and shells were collected and the bombardment began on 3 August. It was a quite sophisticated artillery programme, with shoots spread out along the front, and getting the Germans used to a routine 'hate' around the time of the dawn 'Stand To'. Hill 60 was singled out for special attention and was made to look like the principal target. The French helped with some artillery support, though the sight of a Napoleonic cypher on one of the mortars they provided did not impress the British gunners who saw it!

In another first in the war, 1st King's Shropshire Light Infantry were issued with just seven steel helmets, the very first in the BEF. They reported them to be 'very satisfactory'.

At 2.45 am the British began the 'normal' shelling for thirty minutes. But under its cover men of 16th and 18th Brigades went out into No Man's Land quite close to the enemy line, and bombers used communication trenches to get even closer. As soon as the barrage lifted the British infantry jumped the German front line everywhere. After savage hand-to-hand fighting the crater was recaptured – its slight elevation made it worth the effort.

The 2nd Durham Light Infantry carried out the main attack on the crater. With a strength of thirty-two officers and 1,085 other ranks, the battalion was in fine fettle (though only 180 of the 'originals' who came out in 1914 were left). Excellent patrol work leading up to the attack provided an astonishing amount of accurate detail about the enemy position. Platoons attacked in single waves, with men in the first ranks each carrying 120 rounds of small-arms ammunition (SAA) and four sandbags. In the later waves, considered to have less to do, the men carried 170 rounds SAA, six sandbags and a shovel. Three machine-gun teams went in with each wave; four of them made it through unscathed and set up to consolidate the captured position.

The attack went in at 3.15 am just to the right of the crater and achieved instant success; the carrying parties were all up by 3.40 am and the position was well dug in by 3.55 am. At 4 am ten German prisoners were sent back. At 5.10 a company of East Yorkshires was sent up to reinforce the line, and at 5.35 two companies of Queen's Westminster Rifles were sent up but found they were not really needed. They occupied the old British front line instead. Enemy shelling increased noticeably and caused heavier losses than were sustained in the attack itself.

Losses for 2nd DLI came to six officers and ninety-two men killed; six officers and 262 men wounded; 100 men missing; 466 fell out of the 650 who delivered the attack. It was said by some eyewitnesses that the Durham Light Infantry were looking for the opportunity to avenge the German attacks on Hartlepool in December 1914, where men of their 9th Battalion had the unfortunate distinction of being the first Kitchener volunteers to be killed by enemy action. Some fifty Germans may have been trapped in the crater when it was rushed. Only ten prisoners are recorded. The rest paid the price for the increasing animosity with which the war was being fought. Since the halcyon days of the 'Christmas truce' in 1914 the introduction by the Germans of poison gas, the sinking of civilian ships without warning by submarine, and now flamethrowers was adding greatly to the 'frightfulness' of modern, industrialised warfare.

The RFC did a good job on this fine day, spotting for the guns and suppressing enemy artillery fire. They did it so well that the British could wire in the new position in broad daylight without too much interference. Enemy artillery fire became so heavy that the British had to evacuate some trenches east of Hooge, but German infantry were not able to occupy them either.

Aftermath

—⬥●⬥—

The great historian Cyril Falls, himself a veteran of the war, made this sober appreciation of the battle:

> 'Second Ypres' was, for its size, one of the most murderous battles of the war. The total casualties, including those due to gas, exceeded a hundred thousand, those of the Allies being slightly the greater. By using poison gas in defiance of the convention, the Germans gained the biggest success of the year in the west. They reduced the Ypres Salient to a flat curve just east of the city and secured all the commanding ground. Yet, because their action had been experimental and they had so slender a reserve, they missed a far greater victory before the effect of surprise wore off. Leaving morality out of it, their action was imprudent. It laid them open to heavy reprisals because the prevailing winds were westerly.

Falls reminds us that, at the start of the battle, five British and two French divisions had to withstand the assault of eleven German divisions, who had a vast superiority in artillery, and the shock effect of the new gas weapon. He concluded that one advantage the Germans gained by their assault was to pin down some seven Allied divisions that would have been available for the spring offensives that began on 9 May.

Tactical Developments

The Germans had a marked advantage in that their army corps remained in the same section of the front for a long time. All the corps involved in the battle had served in Flanders since October 1914 and would remain there until the middle of 1916. This gave them a great opportunity to build up their infrastructure, and to become familiar with the terrain. The British tended to move their formations about much more and, especially, divisions were rotated through the corps organisation, with the consequent loss of the possibility of building some continuity of practice and purpose.

The influential (if slightly self-advertising) military commentator, Basil Liddell Hart, was critical of the Germans' failure to exploit the 'easy' victory of the first day:

> The Germans had only to push south for 4 miles to reach Ypres . . . That evening they walked forward 2 miles and then, curiously, stopped . . . Yet on 1st May the Germans had only advanced a few hundred yards further. And when the fighting at last died down, at the end of May, the only outward change was that the nose of the Salient had been flattened – mainly by a voluntary British withdrawal.

After the astonishing opening success of the first gas attacks, the German infantry, 'amazed and euphoric' as they were, soon found themselves on the receiving end of two phenomena – the legendary prowess of the British infantry (and its Lee-Enfield rifle) and a series of recklessly persistent counter-attacks, which added enormously to the Allied casualty lists but did keep the Germans off balance at critical moments. Liddell Hart described the impact of such attacks during the Battle of St Julien:

> This slight taste of repulse sufficed to quench the Germans' thirst for further advance that day. But their irresolution was hidden from the eyes of the British Commanders by the general confusion.

He later emphasised a shift in German tactics towards 'pure siege warfare':

> And during the succeeding days they [the German infantry] were equally content to act as camp-followers to their artillery, merely taking a short step forward to occupy and consolidate such fresh patches of ground as the guns and gas had swept practically clear of defenders . . . For another

month operations were to continue, methodical German attacks answered by unmethodical British attacks.

The carefully limited advance that had been 'short sighted' in the early days was good sense in the later phases of the battle. The full weight of Germany's material superiority in the Salient was used to grind down the opposition.

The British Army fought Second Ypres in exactly the same way as it fought First Ypres. Through a dogged defence it was profligate with the lives of the last of its trained professionals, and sucked in large numbers of the first Territorial formations and draft reserves. The losses sustained in a truly remarkable defence were beyond its control, but the automatic counter-attacks saw casualties mount alarmingly. It was not until after the flame attack at Hooge that a properly considered and organised counter-attack was made.

The British Official History, in its usual measured tone, is severely critical of the hasty, and inevitably ill-organised, counter-attacks that added enormously to the Allied casualty lists. It implies that Sir John French was too much under the influence of Foch, of whom it says:

For ill now, although for weal in the last year of the war, General Foch was the very spirit of the offensive. Sir John French, apart from the desire to conform to his wishes as far as possible, could not fail to be influenced by him; but at heart he was most anxious to withdraw from the impossible position in the Salient and to avoid, if possible, involving the divisions of the New Army in a losing battle as their first experience of war. The struggle at Ypres was therefore continued, and in deference to the French pre-war doctrine of the offensive on all occasions and in all situations, the local commanders, both French and British, were encouraged, nay ordered, to recover by infantry attack the localities they had lost, without even the amount of artillery support which pre-war teaching would have regarded as necessary, let alone what experience had shown to be indispensable.

The year 1915 saw a series of under-resourced and costly British attacks, at Aubers Ridge, Festubert and Loos, when they tried, in the potent words of the Official History, to carry the enemy's breastworks with the bodies of their infantry. As the BEF grew in size and material resources, and took over more responsibility on the Western Front, so it matured in the degree of planning, preparation and training for its assaults. The dreadful experiences of 1915, together with the protracted fighting on the Somme from July to November 1916, combined to transform the BEF into an army so powerful in 1917 and 1918 that it would put the German Army under such intolerable pressure as to lead to Germany's defeat in the field.

While the French troops engaged in the fighting performed with their usual élan, their commanders made elaborate demands on the British and allowed them to carry the brunt of the battle. If they were so anxious to conserve their troops for the Artois spring offensive, they should have said as much in clear and unequivocal terms.

Of the Belgian Army, it is hard to speak too highly. Liddell Hart repeatedly called them 'the hinge of the defence'. This small army, that had lost its recruiting base entirely, fought well in defence of their homeland. They stopped the Germans cold along the canal. If they had given ground there at all, Ypres would have been lost. The Germans could have claimed a victory out of all proportion to the actual ground taken, with significant repercussions in world politics.

Development of Gas and Flame Warfare

As everyone, including the Germans, predicted at the time, the British and French began immediate research and production of the gas weapon. There would be many delays and difficulties organising the necessary industrial techniques and capacity. The British released their first gas cloud at Loos on 25 September 1915, with less than satisfactory results.

On 31 December 1915 the Germans released the first cloud of phosgene gas, which was both less detectable and more toxic than chlorine. Much of the gas used by both sides became a chlorine-phosgene mixture. All armies became increasingly reliant on delivering gas by artillery shell or trench mortar, since gas clouds were so dependent on the wind and there were too many incidents of gas blowing back on the users. A British invention, the Livens

Projector, was first used in October 1916, and entered full production in 1917. It became a very efficient delivery system for large-scale gas attacks, copied by the Germans at the earliest opportunity. The British also developed chemical mixes (using chloropicrin and hydrogen sulphide) that could penetrate German gas masks. Generally the British seem to have developed attack techniques that achieved much higher casualties than those by the Germans. They were, no doubt, assisted by the prevailing westerly winds. Crown Prince Ruprecht's warning that Germany would rue the day she introduced the gas weapon was coming true. As predicted, the Allies were able to divert elements of their powerful industries to gas production. The British produced 6,000 tons in 1916, and doubled that figure in 1917.

In July 1917 Germany added to her stock of 'frightful' weapons with the first use of mustard gas (dichloroethyl sulphide). This gas, that adhered to any exposed skin and caused severe blistering, and which was ruinously fatal to throat and lungs if inhaled, was a particularly detested development. It was especially long-lived, and lingered in bushes and hollows, dug-outs and craters, to cause injury and inconvenience long after its initial discharge. But, like all gas weapons, its primary task was to degrade the enemy's power to resist. The act of forcing the enemy into gas masks for hours at a time is thought to be the chief benefit of using the gas weapon. Saturating artillery battery positions with gas shell was a particularly effective application of this principle.

By November 1918 it was reckoned that sixty-three different gases had been utilised by all combatants.

The British considered developing a flamethrower but early experiments were not a great success. Four enormous devices were deployed for the Somme offensive in 1916, but two were destroyed by shellfire before the 1 July attack, and the others worked properly but were too cumbersome to be of much practical use. Instead they used the serviceable Livens Projector to deliver thermite bombs and containers of oil that burst into flame on contact. Thermite is a pyrotechnic composition of aluminium powder and metal oxide that achieves phenomenal temperatures very quickly. The French produced a man-portable flamethrower, used in 1917 and 1918.

The Germans made great use of their *Flammenwerfers*, adding a lighter, self-igniting version to their armoury. They became an integral part of their stormtroop battalions in 1917 and 1918. They made a total of thirty-two flame attacks in 1915, 160 in 1916, 165 in 1917 and 296 in 1918, when they were widely used in the great spring offensives. The largest single attack utilised 134 weapons all at once. The Germans reckoned these attacks to be 82 per cent successful.

The Morality of Gas Weapons

There is no doubt that Germany gained a great deal of opprobrium by using poison gas first. In 1917 Germany felt the need to publish their official excuse for their use of poison gas on the battlefield. They insisted the French and British had used it against them first. It would be 1926 before Fritz Haber would publicly apologise for this blatant falsehood. It can safely be argued that, if Germany had not introduced poison gas, then it would not have been developed and used by the Western Allies. To illustrate this point we might note that, when the Turks began to suggest that the British had already used gas at Gallipoli, the British immediately recognised the warning that the Germans might initiate its use there. A stockpile of gas, and the experts to use it, were despatched to Gallipoli, but Sir Ian Hamilton made it quite clear that it would never be used unless the Turks did it first.

Eyewitness accounts have expressed the loathing felt for this weapon that produced such agonising death or hideous injury. But another argument asks what is 'clean' or 'gallant' about being mangled by high explosive or shrapnel, or mown down by a machine gun? If war is so dreadful, should it not be fought with every weapon to hand to try to secure a quicker decision and so bring it to an end?

There were a total of 1,286,853 gas casualties in all the armies of the First World War – about 75 per cent caused by gas shell and the rest by gas cloud. Of this total, 93 per cent survived the experience, although 12 per cent would have some sort of permanent disability. But 'only' 7 per cent of the men affected died. Between the wars some distinguished military and scientific thinkers would argue that gas was a more humane weapon than most available in the arsenals of modern war. Furthermore, the 1 1/4 million gas casualties represents only 5 per cent of all casualties inflicted in the war. Could one argue that the result was hardly worth all the economic and military effort involved? Again the cruel arithmetic of war suggests that it took 110 conventional artillery rounds to inflict a casualty, or just sixty-eight gas shells. Logic would suggest the use of more gas, not less.

Deterrence seems to have worked in the Second World War as far as poison gas is concerned. The elaborate provision of anti-gas measures throughout civil and military society, and the stockpiles of weapons for use if the behaviour code was broken, ensured it was not used. The flame weapon, however, was developed into a major asset on the battlefield by all armies.

Conclusion

Second Ypres was never an attempt to break through on the Western Front. It was merely an experiment with a new weapon to make a diversion for troop movements to the East. The local German commanders, having achieved a great success, attempted to collapse the troublesome Salient, with limited results. The Allies should have abandoned their forward defences much sooner, to conserve manpower and ammunition, and to secure a more defensible line. Since German artillery was so close that the town of Ypres was inevitably pulverised out of existence, it can hardly have mattered if the Allied defence lines had been drawn right back to the city walls, flattening out the line and thus eliminating any aspect of a salient and all the difficulties they caused the defenders.

Liddell Hart, having overcome his youthful wartime enthusiasm for generals, became the leading critic of the attritional phase of the war on the Western Front. In the conclusion to his study of Second Ypres he makes this scathing denunciation of the obsession with counter-attacking that so gripped the French and British higher commanders in 1915:

> To throw away good money after bad is foolish. But to throw away men's lives where there is no reasonable chance of advantage is criminal. In the heat of battle mistakes in the command are inevitable and amply excusable. But the real indictment of leadership arises when attacks that are inherently vain are ordered merely because if they succeed

they would be useful. For such manslaughter, whether it springs from ignorance, a false conception of war or want of moral courage, commanders should be held accountable to the nation.

Setting aside the devotion to duty shown by the officers and men of all the nations involved in Second Ypres, this harsh judgement should stand as an indictment of two men in particular: Ferdinand Foch and Sir John French.

Appendices

Appendix I: Orders of Battle

British Expeditionary Force
General Headquarters
Commander-in-Chief: Field Marshal Sir John French
Chief of the General Staff: Lieutenant General Sir William Robertson

Second Army
Commander: General Sir Horace Smith-Dorrien (to 7 May 1915)
Lieutenant General Sir Herbert Plumer (from 7 May 1915)
Major General, General Staff: George F. Milne

II CORPS
General Officer Commanding: Lieutenant General Sir Charles Ferguson
Brigadier General, General Staff: W. T. Furse

5th Division (Major General H. F. M. Morland)
13th Brigade (Brigadier General R. Wanless O'Gowan)
2nd KOSB
1st R. West Kent
2nd Duke of Wellington's
2nd KOYLI
9th London – Queen Victoria's Rifles (TF)

14th Brigade (Brigadier General G. H. Thesiger)
1st Devonshire
1st DCLI
1st East Surrey

2nd Manchester
5th Cheshire (TF)

15th Brigade (Brigadier General E. Northey)
1st Norfolk
1st Cheshire
1st Bedfordshire
1st Dorsetshire
6th King's (TF)

Royal Field Artillery Brigades
XV (52, 80 Batteries)
XXVII (119, 120, 121 Batteries)
XXVIII (122, 123, 124 Batteries)
130th Battery of XXX Howitzer Brigade

Field Companies, Royal Engineers
59th, 2nd Home Counties (TF), 1st North Midlands (TF)

Mounted Troops
C Squadron, Northants Yeomanry
One Cyclist Company

V CORPS
General Officer Commanding: Lieutenant General Sir Herbert Plumer (to 8 May 1915)
Lieutenant General Sir Edward Allenby (from 8 May 1915)
Brigadier General, General Staff: H. S. Jeudwine

4th Division (Major General H. F. M. Wilson)
10th Brigade (Brigadier General C. Hull)
1st R. Warwickshire
1st R. Irish Fusiliers
2nd Seaforth Highlanders
2nd R. Dublin Fusiliers
7th Argyll & Sutherland Highlanders (TF)

11th Brigade (Brigadier General J. Hasler)
1st Somerset Light Infantry
1st Hampshire

1st East Lancashire
1st Rifle Brigade
5th London – London Rifle Brigade (TF)

12th Brigade (Brigadier General F. Anley)
1st King's Own
2nd Lancashire Fusiliers
2nd Essex
2nd Royal Irish
5th South Lancashire (TF)
2nd Monmouth (TF)

RFA Brigades
XIV (68, 88 Batteries)
XXIX (125, 126, 127 Batteries)
XXXII (27, 134, 135 Batteries)

RGA
2nd Mountain Battery

Field Companies RE
9th, 1st West Lancashire (TF)

Mounted Troops
A Squadron, Northants Yeomanry
One Cyclist company

27th Division (Major General T. D. O. Snow)
80th Brigade (Brigadier General W. Smith)
2nd KSLI
3rd KRRC
4th KRRC
4th Rifle Brigade
Princess Patricia's Canadian Light Infantry

81st Brigade (Brigadier General H. Croker)
1st Royal Scots
2nd Cameron Highlanders
2nd Gloucestershire
1st Argyll & Sutherland Highlanders

9th Royal Scots (TF)
9th Argyll & Sutherland Highlanders (TF)

82nd Brigade (Brigadier General J. Longley)
1st Royal Irish
2nd R. Irish Fusiliers
2nd DCLI
1st Leinster
1st Cambridgeshire (TF)

RFA Brigades (All 4-gun batteries except 61st Howitzer)
I (11, 98, 132, 133 Batteries)
XIX (39, 59, 96, 131 Batteries)
XX (67, 99, 148, 364 Batteries)
61st Battery (VII Howitzer Brigade)

Field Companies RE
17th, 1st Wessex (TF), 2nd Wessex (TF)

Mounted troops
A Squadron Surrey Yeomanry
One Cyclist company

28th Division (Major General E. S. Bulfin)
83rd Brigade (Brigadier General R. Boyle)
2nd King's Own
1st KOYLI
2nd East Yorkshire
1st York & Lancaster
5th King's Own (TF)
3rd Monmouth (TF)

84th Brigade (Brigadier General L. Bols)
2nd Northumberland Fusiliers
1st Suffolk
2nd Cheshire
1st Welch
12th London (Rangers) (TF)
1st Monmouth (TF)

Appendices

85th Brigade (Brigadier General A. Chapman)
2nd Buffs
3rd Royal Fusiliers
2nd East Surrey
3rd Middlesex
8th Middlesex (TF)

RFA Brigades (All 4-gun batteries, except Howitzers)
III (18, 22, 62, 365 Batteries)
XXXI (69, 100, 103, 118 Batteries)
CXLVI (75, 149, 366, 367 Batteries)
37, 65 Batteries (VIII Howitzer Brigade)

Field Companies RE
38th, 1st Northumbrian (TF)

Mounted Troops
B Squadron Surrey Yeomanry
One Cyclist company

50th (1st Northumbrian) Division (TF) (Major General Sir W. Lindsay)
149th (1st Northumberland) Brigade (Brigadier General J. Riddell)
4th Northumberland Fusiliers
5th Northumberland Fusiliers
6th Northumberland Fusiliers
7th Northumberland Fusiliers

150th (1st York and Durham) Brigade (Brigadier General J. Bush)
4th East Yorkshire
5th Durham Light Infantry
4th and 5th Green Howards

151st (1st Durham LI) Brigade (Brigadier General H. Martin)
6th Durham Light Infantry
7th Durham Light Infantry
8th Durham Light Infantry
9th Durham Light Infantry

RFA Brigades (15-pounder guns and 5-inch Howitzers)
1st Northumbrian

2nd Northumbrian
3rd Northumbrian
4th Northumbrian (Howitzer)

Field Company RE
2nd Northumbrian

Mounted Troops
A Squadron Yorkshire Hussars
One Cyclist company

*

British infantry divisions also contained three field ambulances, a signals company, a mobile veterinary section, a divisional ammunition column and a divisional transport 'train'.

*

1st Canadian Division (Lieutenant General E. A. Alderson)
1st Canadian Brigade (Brigadier General M. Mercer)
1st Battalion (Western Ontario)
2nd Battalion (Eastern Ontario)
3rd Battalion (Toronto)
4th Battalion

2nd Canadian Brigade (Brigadier General Arthur Currie)
5th Battalion (Western Cavalry)
7th Battalion (1st British Columbia)
8th Battalion (Winnipeg Rifles)
10th Battalion

3rd Canadian Brigade (Brigadier General R. Turner, VC)
13th Battalion (R. Highlanders of Canada)
14th Battalion (Royal Montreal)
15th Battalion (48th Highlanders of Canada)
16th Battalion (Canadian Scottish)

Canadian FA Brigades (4-gun batteries)
I (1, 2, 3, 4 Batteries)
II (5, 6, 7, 8 Batteries)
III (9, 10, 11, 12 Batteries)

RFA Brigade
CXVIII (Howitzer) 458 & 459 Howitzer Batteries
Canadian Engineer Field Companies 1, 2 & 3
Mounted Troops
Service Squadron 19th Alberta Dragoons
One Cyclist company

Lahore Division: Major General H. Keary
Ferozepore Brigade (Brigadier General R. Egerton)
Connaught Rangers
9th Bhopal Infantry
57th Wilde's Rifles
129th Baluchis
4th London – Royal Fusiliers (TF)

Jullundur Brigade (Brigadier General E. Strickland)
1st Manchester
40th Pathans
47th Sikhs
59th Scinde Rifles
4th Suffolks (TF)

Sirhind Brigade (Brigadier General W. Walker, VC)
1st Highland Light Infantry
15th Sikhs
1/1st Gurkhas
1/4th Gurkhas
4th King's (Special Reserve)

RFA Brigades
V (64, 73, 81 Batteries)
XI (83, 84, 85 Batteries)
XVIII (59, 93, 94 Batteries)
XLIII (How.) 40 & 47 Batteries

Engineers
20th and 21st Companies
3rd Sappers and Miners

Pioneers
34th Sikh Pioneers

Mounted Troops
15th Lancers

Corps Heavy Artillery (at 22 April 1915 – 4.7-inch guns)
2nd London Heavy Battery (XIII Brigade RGA)
1st North Midlands Heavy Battery (XIII Brigade RGA)
122nd Heavy Battery (XI Brigade RGA)
123rd Heavy Battery

Cavalry Corps
General Officer Commanding: Lieutenant General E. Allenby (to 4 May 1915)
Lieutenant General Hon. Sir Julian Byng (from 4 May)
Brigadier General, General Staff: P. Howell

1st Cavalry Division (Major General H. de Lisle)
1st Cavalry Brigade (Brigadier General C. Briggs)
Queen's Bays
5th Dragoon Guards
11th Hussars

2nd Cavalry Brigade (Brigadier General R. Mullens)
4th Dragoon Guards
9th Lancers

9th Cavalry Brigade (Brigadier General W. Greenly)
15th Hussars
19th Hussars

RHA Brigade
VII (H, I & 1st Warwickshire (TF) Batteries)

Field Squadron RE: No. 1

2nd Cavalry Division (Major General C. Kavanagh)
3rd Cavalry Brigade (Brigadier General J. Vaughan)
4th Hussars
5th Lancers
16th Lancers

4th Cavalry Brigade (Brigadier General C. Bingham)
6th Dragoon Guards
3rd Hussars
Oxfordshire Hussars (TF)

5th Cavalry Brigade (Brigadier General Sir P. W. Chetwode)
Royal Scots Greys
12th Lancers
20th Hussars

RHA Brigade
III (D, E, J Batteries)

Field Squadron RE: No. 2

3rd Cavalry Division (Major General Hon. Julian Byng)
6th Cavalry Brigade (Brigadier General D. Campbell)
3rd Dragoon Guards
1st Royal Dragoons
N. Somerset Yeomanry

7th Cavalry Brigade (Brigadier General A. Kennedy)
1st Life Guards
2nd Life Guards
Leicester Yeomanry

8th Cavalry Brigade (Brigadier General C. Bulkeley-Johnson)
Royal Horse Guards
10th Hussars

RHA Brigade
XV (C, K, G Batteries)

Field Squadron RE: No. 3

Royal Flying Corps
Second Wing
1st Squadron
5th Squadron
6th Squadron

*

French Troops
DÉTACHEMENT D'ARMÉE DE BELGIQUE (GENERAL HENRI PUTZ)
18th Division (General Lefèvre)

35th Brigade
32nd Infantry Regiment
66th Infantry Regiment

36th Brigade
77th Infantry Regiment
135th Infantry Regiment

Three *groupes* of 75mm artillery
One squadron cavalry

45th (Algerian) Division (General Quiquandon)
90th Brigade
2nd *bis* Zouaves de Marche
1st Tirailleurs de Marche
1st Battalion d'Afrique
3rd Battalion d'Afrique

91st Brigade
7th Zouaves de Marche
3rd *bis* Zouaves de Marche

Three *groupes* of 75mm artillery
One squadron 1st Regiment de Marche de Chasseurs d'Afrique

152nd Division (General Joppé)
304th Brigade
268th Infantry Regiment
290th Infantry Regiment

4th Moroccan Brigade
1st Moroccan Infantry
8th Tirailleurs de Marche

Two *groupes* of 75mm artillery
Two squadrons cavalry

153rd Division (General Deligny)
306th Brigade
418th Infantry Regiment
2nd Battalion Chasseurs à Pied
4th Battalion Chasseurs à Pied

3rd Moroccan Brigade
1st Mixte Zouaves et Tirailleurs
9th Zouaves de Marche

Two *groupes* of 90mm artillery
One *groupe* (2 batteries) of 95mm artillery
Two squadrons cavalry

87th Territorial Division (General Roy)
173rd Brigade
73rd Territorial Regiment
74th Territorial Regiment

174th Brigade
76th Territorial Regiment
79th Territorial Regiment
80th Territorial Regiment

186th Brigade
100th Territorial Regiment
102nd Territorial Regiment

Two *groupes* of 90mm artillery
Two squadrons 4th Dragoons

Heavy Artillery (available on 22 April 1915)
Two batteries 120mm guns

*

Belgian Troops
6th Infantry Division (Lieutenant General A.-L. de Ceuninck)
18th Mixed Brigade (Major-General Maes)
1st Grenadiers
2nd Grenadiers (temporarily composited – 4 battalions)
18th Machine-gun Company
One artillery battalion (3 batteries)
One platoon mounted Gensdarmes

19th Mixed Brigade
1st Carabiniers
3rd Carabiniers
19th Machine-gun Company
One artillery battalion (3 batteries)
One platoon mounted Gensdarmes

20th Mixed Brigade
2nd Carabiniers
4th Carabiniers
20th Machine-gun Company
One artillery battalion (3 batteries)
One platoon mounted Gensdarmes

Divisional Troops
1st Chasseurs à Cheval
6th Artillery Regiment
6th Battalion Divisional Engineers
6th Section Field Telegraphy
Transport Corps

1st Infantry Division (Lieutenant General Baix)
2nd Mixed Brigade
2nd Line Infantry
22nd Line Infantry
2nd Machine-gun Company
One artillery battalion (3 batteries)
One platoon mounted Gensdarmes

3rd Mixed Brigade

3rd Line Infantry
23rd Line Infantry
3rd Machine-gun Company
One artillery battalion (3 batteries)
One platoon mounted Gensdarmes

4th Mixed brigade
4th Line Infantry
24th Line Infantry
4th Machine-gun Company
One artillery battalion (3 batteries)
One platoon mounted Gensdarmes

Divisional Troops
3rd Lancers
1st Artillery Regiment
1st Battalion Divisional Engineers
1st Section Field Telegraphy
Transport Corps

*

German Troops
Fourth Army
Commander: General Duke Albrecht of Württemberg
Chief of Staff: Major General Emil Ilse
XV Corps (General Berthold von Deimling)
30th Infantry Division

60th Brigade
99th Infantry Regiment
143rd Infantry Regiment

85th Brigade
105th Infantry Regiment
136th Infantry Regiment

30th Artillery Brigade
51st Artillery Regiment
85th Artillery Regiment

Divisional Troops
1st Field Company, 1st Battalion, 15th Pioneers
30th Pontoon Engineers
30th Telegraph Detachment

39th Infantry Division
61st Brigade
126th Infantry Regiment
132nd Infantry Regiment

82nd Brigade
171st Infantry Regiment
172nd Infantry Regiment

39th Artillery Brigade
66th Artillery Regiment
80th Artillery Regiment

Divisional Troops
2nd and 3rd Field Company, 1st Battalion, 15th Pioneers
39th Pontoon Engineers
39th Telegraph Detachment

Additional Artillery
Four 8-inch Howitzers
Twelve 5.9-inch Howitzers
Four 5.2-inch guns
Two 4-inch guns
Fourteen old or captured guns

XXII RESERVE CORPS (GENERAL VON FALKENHAYN)
43rd Reserve Infantry Division

85th Reserve Brigade
201st Reserve Infantry Regiment
202nd Reserve Infantry Regiment

86th Reserve Brigade
203rd Reserve Infantry Regiment

204th Reserve Infantry Regiment

15th Reserve Jäger Battalion

Divisional Troops
43rd Field Artillery Regiment
43rd Reserve Pioneer Company
43rd Reserve Pontoon Engineers
43rd Reserve Ambulance Company
43rd Reserve Cavalry Detachment

44th Reserve Infantry Division (part)
88th Reserve Brigade
207th Reserve Infantry Regiment

XXIII Reserve Corps (General Hugo von Kathen)
45th Reserve Infantry Division

89th Reserve Brigade
209th Reserve Infantry Regiment
212th Reserve Infantry Regiment

90th Reserve Brigade
210th Reserve Infantry Regiment
211th Reserve Infantry Regiment

17th Reserve Jäger Battalion

Divisional Troops
45th Field Artillery Regiment
45th Reserve Pioneer Company
45th Reserve Pontoon Engineers
45th Reserve Ambulance Company
45th Reserve Cavalry Detachment

46th Reserve Infantry Division
91st Reserve Brigade
213th Reserve Infantry Regiment
214th Reserve Infantry Regiment

92nd Reserve Brigade

215th Reserve Infantry Regiment
216th Reserve Infantry Regiment

18th Reserve Jäger Battalion

Divisional Troops
46th Field Artillery Regiment
46th Reserve Pioneer Company
46th Reserve Pontoon Engineers
46th Reserve Ambulance Company
46th Reserve Cavalry Detachment

XXVI RESERVE CORPS (GENERAL OTTO FREIHERR VON HÜGEL)
51st Reserve Infantry Division
101st Reserve Brigade
233rd Reserve Infantry Regiment
234th Reserve Infantry Regiment

102nd Reserve Brigade
235th Reserve Infantry Regiment
236th Reserve Infantry Regiment

23rd Reserve Jäger Battalion

Divisional Troops
51st Field Artillery Regiment
Mobile Ersatz Detachment 26th Field Artillery Regiment
51st Reserve Pioneer Company
51st Reserve Pontoon Engineers
51st Reserve Ambulance Company
51st Reserve Cavalry Detachment

52nd Reserve Infantry Division
103rd Reserve Brigade
237th Reserve Infantry Regiment
238th Reserve Infantry Regiment

104th Reserve Brigade
239th Reserve Infantry Regiment
240th Reserve Infantry Regiment

24th Reserve Jäger Battalion

Divisional Troops
52nd Field Artillery Regiment
52nd Reserve Pioneer Company
52nd Reserve Pontoon Engineers
52nd Reserve Ambulance Company
52nd Reserve Cavalry Detachment

Attached Troops
37th Landwehr Brigade
73rd Landwehr Infantry Regiment
74th Landwehr Infantry Regiment

2nd Reserve Ersatz Brigade
3rd Reserve Ersatz Infantry Regiment
4th Reserve Ersatz Infantry Regiment

XXVII Reserve Corps (General von Carlowitz)
53rd (Saxon) Reserve Infantry Division
105th Reserve Brigade
241st Reserve Infantry Regiment
242nd Reserve Infantry Regiment

106th Reserve Brigade
243rd Reserve Infantry Regiment
244th Reserve Infantry Regiment

25th Reserve Jäger Battalion

Divisional Troops
53rd Field Artillery Regiment
53rd Reserve Pioneer Company
53rd Reserve Pontoon Engineers
53rd Reserve Ambulance Company
53rd Reserve Cavalry Detachment

54th (Württemberg) Reserve Infantry Division
107th Reserve Brigade
245th Reserve Infantry Regiment
246th Reserve Infantry Regiment

108th Reserve Brigade
247th Infantry Regiment
248th Reserve Infantry Regiment

28th Reserve Jäger Battalion

Divisional Troops
54th Field Artillery Regiment
Ersatz Abteilung 59th Field Artillery Regiment
54th Reserve Pioneer Company
54th Reserve Pontoon Engineers
54th Reserve Ambulance Company
54th Reserve Cavalry Detachment

Attached Troops
38th Landwehr Brigade
77th Landwehr Infantry Regiment
78th Landwehr Infantry Regiment

Additional Artillery available to XXIII, XXVI and XXVII Reserve Corps
One 17-inch howitzer ('Big Bertha')
Twenty 8-inch howitzers
Seventy-two 5.9-inch howitzers
Four 5.2-inch guns
Sixteen 4-inch guns
Thirty-four old or captured guns

Additional Troops
2nd Marine Brigade
2nd Marine Regiment (only)

4th Marine Brigade
4th Matrosen Regiment
5th Matrosen Regiment

Appendix II: Casualties

British Casualties – Second Ypres 1915

Unit	Officers			Other Ranks			Total
	Killed	Wounded	Missing	Killed	Wounded	Missing	
1st Cavalry Division	17	59	9	151	638	329	1203
2nd Cavalry Division	4	7	-	36	180	17	244
3rd Cavalry Division	31	60	3	273	1057	194	1618
4th Division	87	224	36	1566	5476	3470	10859
5th Division	71	209	13	1068	5478	1155	7994
27th Division	55	166	13	1122	4980	927	7263
28th Division	97	300	98	3177	5548	6313	15533
50th Division	40	121	25	596	2963	1459	5204
Canadian Division	65	104	39	1672	1822	1767	5469
Lahore Division (British)	28	105	-	180	1096	345	1754
(Indian)	6	57	1	177	1684	209	2134
Grand Total	501	1412	237	10018	30922	16185	59275

From the British Official History.

German Casualties – Second Ypres 1915

Unit: XV Corps						
	Officers			Other Ranks		
Dates	Killed	Wounded	Missing	Killed	Wounded	Missing
21–30 April	7	10	1	101	437	28
1–10 May	13	26	-	269	900	15
11–20 May	3	6	-	129	397	4
21–30 May	8	13	1	123	488	28
Totals	31	55	2	622	2222	75

Unit: XXII Reserve Corps						
	Officers			Other Ranks		
Dates	Killed	Wounded	Missing	Killed	Wounded	Missing
21–30 April	40	89	13	977	3862	1780
1–10 May	3	8	-	141	524	-
11–20 May	14	23	5	299	1349	515
21–30 May	40	89	13	977	3861	1780
Totals	97	209	31	2394	9596	4075

Unit: XXVI Reserve Corps						
	Officers			Other Ranks		
Dates	Killed	Wounded	Missing	Killed	Wounded	Missing
21–30 April	59	124	4	1002	4268	813
1–10 May	19	45	2	519	2408	208
11–20 May	14	20	2	380	1079	323
21–30 May	58	119	4	998	4247	813
Totals	150	308	12	2899	12002	2157

Unit: XXVII Reserve Corps						
	Officers			Other Ranks		
Dates	Killed	Wounded	Missing	Killed	Wounded	Missing
21–30 April	16	38	2	319	1121	144
1–10 May	24	121	–	660	2785	74
11–20 May	4	21	2	346	1120	185
21–30 May	16	38	2	319	1121	144
Totals	60	218	6	1644	6147	547

Sub totals					
Officers			Other Ranks		
Killed	Wounded	Missing	Killed	Wounded	Missing
338	790	51	7559	29967	6854
Grand Totals					
Officers			Other Ranks		
1179			44380		

Reported every ten days. From an Intelligence File in British Second Army papers.

*

Note: this table differs in minor detail from that in the Official History, but no two lists of casualties ever agree. The major difference is that it includes all of XXII Reserve Corps, of which only a part was engaged in the battles against the British at Second Ypres, but was much engaged by the French and Belgians. Neither list gives the losses of the Marine Corps heavily engaged.

The Official History summarises the total German loss as 860 officers and 34,073 other ranks.

Losses for 37th Landwehr and 2nd Ersatz Reserve Brigades are included in XXVI Reserve Corps, and for 38th Landwehr Brigade in XXVII Reserve Corps.

Bibliography

Arthur, Max, *Symbol of Courage: A Complete History of the Victoria Cross*, Macmillan 2004.

Atkinson, C. T., *The Royal Hampshire Regiment Vol. 2 1914–1918*, 1952.

Ballard, Brig. Gen. C., *Smith-Dorrien*, Constable 1931.

Beckett, Ian, *Ypres: The First Battle 1914*, Pearson Longman 2004.

Berkeley, R., MC, *History of the Rifle Brigade in the War of 1914–18 Vol. 1*, 1926.

Bond, R. C., *The King's Own Yorkshire Light Infantry in the Great War*, Humphries 1919.

Cave, Nigel, *Sanctuary Wood and Hooge*, Leo Cooper 1995.

Corrigan, Gordon, *Sepoys in the Trenches*, Spellmount 1999.

Crookenden, Arthur, *History of the Cheshire Regiment in the Great War*, published privately n.d.

Dancocks, Daniel, *Gallant Canadians: The Story of the 10th Canadian Infantry Battalion 1914–1919*, Alberta, Canada 1990.

Dixon, Janet & John, *With Rifle and Pick* (3rd Monmouths), CWM Press 1991.

Edmonds, Brig. Gen. J.E., *History of the Great War: Military Operations: France and Belgium 1915, Vol. I*, Macmillan 1927.

Falls, Cyril, *The First World War*, Longmans 1960.

Geoghan, Brig. Gen. S., *Campaigns and History of the Royal Irish Regiment from 1900 to 1922*, Naval and Military Press reprint 2007.

Gillon, Captain Stair, *The K. O. S. B. in the Great War*, Nelson 1930.

Grimwade, F. Clive, *War History of 4th Battalion London Regiment (Royal Fusiliers) 1914–1919*, 4th London Regimental Headquarters 1922.

Haber, L. F., *The Poisonous Cloud: Chemical Warfare in the First World War*, Clarendon Press Oxford 1986.

Bibliography

Hare, Major-General Sir Stuart, *Annals of the King's Royal Rifle Corps Vol. V*, John Murray 1932.

Hodder-Williams, Ralph, *Princess Patricia's Canadian Light Infantry 1914–1918: Vol. 1*, Hodder & Stoughton 1923.

Hogg, Ian V., *Gas*, Ballantine 1975.

Holmes, Richard, *The Little Field Marshal: Sir John French*, Cape 1981.

Holt, Major and Mrs, *Ypres Salient: A Battlefield Guide*, Leo Cooper 1996/2003.

Jones, Simon, *World War I Gas Warfare: Tactics and Equipment*, Osprey 2007.

Jourdain, Lt. Col. H. & Fraser, E., *The Connaught Rangers Vol. 1*, Schull Books, Cork 1999.

Keeson, Major C., *History and Records of Queen Victoria's Rifles 1792–1922*, Constable 1923.

Lambrecht, Eddy, *Gas Clouds over Flanders: Second Battle of Ypres*, G.H. Smith 2005.

Liddell Hart, Basil, *History of the First World War*, Cassell 1934.

Macdonald, Lyn, *1915: Death of Innocence*, Headline 1993.

Merewether, Lt. Col. J. W. B. and Smith, The Right Hon. Sir Frederick, *The Indian Corps in France*, John Murray 1917.

Moody, R. S. H., *Historical Records of the Buffs (East Kent Regiment) 1914–1919*, Medici Society 1932.

Moore, William, *Gas Attack: Chemical Warfare 1915 to the Present Day*, Leo Cooper 1987.

Murphy, Lt. Col. C., *History of the Suffolk Regiment 1914–1927*, Hutchinson 1928.

O'Neill, H. C., *Royal Fusiliers in the Great War*, Heinemann 1922.

Passingham, Ian, *All the Kaiser's Men: The Life and Death of the German Army on the Western Front 1914–1918*, Sutton 2003.

Pearce, Col. H. & Sloman, Brig. Gen. H., *History of the East Surrey Regiment, Vol. II 1914–1917*, Medici Society 1923.

Perry, Nicholas, *Major General Oliver Nugent and the Ulster Division 1915–1918*, Army Records Society 2007.

Raimes, Major A., *Fifth Battalion The Durham Light Infantry 1914–1918*, Regimental Committee 1931.

Sandilands, Brigadier H. R., *The Fifth in the Great War: History of the First and Second Northumberland Fusiliers 1914–18*, Grigg & Son 1938.

Shephard, Ernest, *A Sergeant-Major's War: From Hill 60 to the Somme*, Bird Crowood 1988.

Simpson, Maj.-Gen. C. R., *History of the Lincolnshire Regiment*

1914–1918, Medici Society 1931.

Smith-Dorrien, General Sir Horace, *Memories of Forty-Eight Years' Service*, John Murray 1925.

Spagnoly, Tony and Smith, Tom, *Salient Points Three*, Leo Cooper 2001.

U. S. War Office, *Histories of the 251 Divisions of the German Army that Participated in the War 1914–1918*, US War Dept. Washington 1920.

Various Authorities, *Canada in the Great World War Vol. III: Guarding the Channel Ports*, United Publishers of Canada, Toronto 1919.

Veitch, Major E. H., *8th Battalion The Durham Light Infantry*, Veitch & Sons 1927.

Ward, Dudley, *History of the Dorsetshire Regiment 1914–1919: 1st Battalion*, Henry Ling 1932.

Wheeler-Holoran, Capt. A. and Wyatt, Capt. G., *The Rangers' Historical Records: From 1859 to the Conclusion of the Great War*, Harrison 1921.

Whitton, Lt. Col. F. E., *History of the Prince of Wales's Leinster Regiment (Royal Canadians)*, Schull Books, Cork 1998.

Williams, Jeffery, *First in the Field: Gault of the Patricias*, Leo Cooper 1995.

Wood, Major W. de B., *History of the King's Shropshire Light Infantry in the Great War 1914–1918*, Medici Society 1925.

Wylly, Col. H. C., *Crown and Company: The Historical Records of 2nd Battn. Royal Dublin Fusiliers Vol. II 1911–1922*, Gale and Polden 1923.

Wyrall, Everard, *History of the Duke of Cornwall's Light Infantry 1914–1919*, Methuen 1932.

Wyrall, Everard, *The Die Hards in the Great War Vol. 1 1914–1916*, (Middlesex Regiment) Harrison & Sons 1926.

Wyrall, Everard, *The East Yorkshire Regiment in the Great War 1914–1918*, Harrison 1928.

Wyrall, Everard, *History of the 50th Division 1914–1919*, Lund Humphries 1939.

Index

Index

The Gas Attacks: Ypres 1915